GERSHWIN

Text by Florence Stevenson De Santis

Edited by Florence Stevenson De Santis

Book Design by Albert Karsten

Published by Treves Publishing Company, a Division of
Elite Publishing Corporation
120 East 56th Street
New York, New York 10022

Library of Congress Catalog Card Number: 86-21320
ISBN 0-918367-18-2

Portraits of Greatness: Trade Mark Reg. No. 1,368,932

Printed and bound by
Boulanger, Inc.
Montreal, Canada

These pages: George and Ira Gershwin, Hollywood, 1930
Gershwin Collection, Library of Congress, Washington, D.C.

Cover: *Self-Portrait by George Gershwin*;
Photograph by Randy Leffingwell.

Portraits of Greatness ®
Published series of pictorial biographies
Series I* Verdi
        Mozart
        Beethoven
        Chopin
        Dante
(First published in Italian under the title "I Grandi Di Tutti I
Tempi," copyright 1965, Arnoldo Mondadori Editore, SpA,
Milan.)

Series II** Puccini
        Rossini
        Respighi
        Giordano
        Gershwin
        Toscanini
(By Treves Publishing Company, a division of Elite Publishing
Company. Each volume and title series copyrighted.)

PORTRAITS OF GREATNESS

GERSHWIN

by Florence Stevenson De Santis

*To my father, an early player
and champion of George Gershwin's music,
who would have loved this book.*

**TREVES
PUBLISHING
COMPANY**

GEORGE GERSHWIN

George Gershwin once summed up his own life by writing, "My people are American—my time is now." Fifty years after his death, that statement stands as the best description of his personality and genius.

He lives today as vividly as he did in his own time, the youthful symbol of a youthful century. His music has grown in appeal with every passing year. Even his opera, which he intended for the Metropolitan Opera in New York, has arrived there. George would have been pleased, but not really surprised. He always knew when his work was good.

A NEW YORK BOYHOOD

When George Gershwin was born, the vast changes ahead for his world were undreamed of. On September 26, 1898, the Gershwin house at 242 Snediker Avenue, Brooklyn, stood in an area still semi-rural. He didn't remember it, however, as the family moved back to Manhattan when he was two, and he grew up in the heart of the city.

It is strange to realize that this symbol of the coming Jazz Age was actually born in the Victorian era, when Queen Victoria herself still had three years to live. In 1898 the Spanish-American War was fought, making Theodore Roosevelt, once Police Commissioner of New York, a military hero. The Klondike gold rush sent thousands to Alaska. William McKinley was president of a country seething with industrial expansion—and farm unrest.

New York, too, was bursting at the seams. New York was filling with immigrants pouring in to get away from East European persecution and southern European poverty. "The streets were paved with gold," they said, and if thousands crowded into New York slums found it not so, many others sniffed opportunity in the very air of this brash, expansive country.

Although Victorian social standards still ruled, change was in the air. Women wore long skirts, but donned pants to ride the bicycle, whose reinvention as a vehicle with wheels the same size had created a bicycle craze. Charles Dana Gibson drew

Left: in 1963, the youngest Gershwin brother, Arthur, and sister Frances unveiled a plaque marking the Brooklyn house in which George Gershwin was born. Lower right: the house, now gone, as it appeared in 1963. Changing lifestyles at the turn of the century created the "New Woman," who participated in outdoor sports and recreation. Upper right: Charles Dana Gibson drew some of his famous "Gibson Girls" in the new bathing dresses of 1900. Lower left, fashionable pants costume for the 1890's bicycling craze.

Upper right: Ira Gershwin at about eight years old. Left: lower Fifth Avenue strollers, about 1896, the year he was born. Below: a member of the "Broadway Squad" directs a stranger, at Broadway and Fulton Street in 1898, with Trinity Church in the background. This *special police group, all at least six feet tall, were posted at every important corner from Bowling Green to Forty-Second Street, to control traffic and aid the masses of people entering New York life from every country. With no traffic lights, traffic was already a problem!*

David Belasco, producer, left below, dominated the theater in Gershwin's boyhood with his "sensational" subject matter and elaborately realistic productions, often writing the plays he produced. His one-act "Madame Butterfly" and full-length "Girl of the Golden West" became the libretti for two Puccini operas. Right: Richard

Mansfield, leading dramatic star, in makeup for "Cyrano de Bergerac," which he brought to this country in 1898. Bottom, Rose Gershwin with the three boys and the "maid," probably in Prospect Park, Brooklyn, about 1901. Ira sits in front of Rose, George between her and the "maid," and Arthur to the left.

a new ideal girl, who went sailing and played tennis. Inventions excited everyone, with Thomas Edison a national idol. His Edison Home Model of a cylinder phonograph had been followed by the kinetoscope, which showed short moving picture sequences, and both could be used for a penny each in entertainment arcades.

The New York theater flourished, with plays ranging from crude melodramas to Shakespearean productions by actor-managers who headed their own companies. Playwrights included William Gillette, who was to create the stage Sherlock Holmes in 1899, James A. Herne, Clyde Fitch, Augustus Thomas and David Belasco. Highly popular music hall stars included Harrigan & Hart, Weber & Fields, and Lillian Russell.

Musically, the Nineties fermented, too. The Metropolitan Opera was fourteen years old, and there were a number of orchestral ensembles. The classical music establishment debated the new "dissonance" influences from Europe, where serious young musicians went to study. Columbia University, along with Harvard, led the academic musical establishment, which sought to create an "American" school, but really wanted to continue with nineteenth-century European romanticism.

Popular music, influenced by a wish to be respectable, was dominated by highly sentimental songs, often called ballads, which did require a trained voice to sing. But from the declining form of entertainment called the minstrel show a new influence had appeared. Dubbed "ragtime," this saucy black-invented music had been spreading ever since it was widely heard at the Chicago World's Fair of 1893. By the year 1911, when young Irving Berlin wrote "Alexander's Ragtime Band," he was almost too late—"jazz" had arrived.

The stage musical in New York had a new name, too, "musical comedy," but it was really an American form of European operetta. In the year of George Gershwin's birth, Victor Herbert wrote "The Fortune Teller" while still conductor of the Pittsburgh Symphony Orchestra. He was to dominate the form, and even to cross Gershwin's life at a later important moment.

Below: a rare photo of all three Gershwin boys, 1912, with Ira, George and Arthur, left to right. The girl is their cousin, Rose Lagowitz, at whose family's Brighton Beach, Brooklyn post card shop Ira worked that summer. Coney Island, next-door to Brighton Beach, was then a flourishing resort for city dwellers, who came by trolley car to enjoy the sea air, the famous restaurants, some of them open-air gardens, and the many thrilling rides. Bottom: the "Tunnel of Love," whose cars wound through dark grottoes, very popular with couples for "spooning."

Into this rich world of exciting events and people, George Gershwin was born. He already had the brother who was to be so closely associated with him, as Ira was born in 1896. After George came Arthur in 1900, and the one girl, Frances, in 1907.

They are all important, because the Gershwins were always to be a closely knit family, either living together or close by each other. Nothing could be more American—or New York—in that time than the fact that the parents were both immigrants. They were Russian Jews of middle-class standing, not confined to the Pale of Settlement, as most Jews in Russia were by law. Moishe Gershovitz' father was a gun expert in the Czar's artillery. Rose Bruskin's father was a furrier, and both families lived in St. Petersburg, a fact Rose was always to emphasize.

Moishe Gershovitz, "leather worker" on his passport, left Russia to avoid the army and to follow Rose, who had already gone to the United States with her family. It is recorded of him that he leaned too far over the ship's rail to see the Statue of Liberty and lost his hat to the wind. In the hat band was a slip of paper with the address of a tailor uncle in New York. But in those days Moishe could easily find Yiddish or Russian speakers in the city, and unfazed, he finally discovered "Greenstein the tailor" in Brooklyn.

It was an incident typical of his American career. Moishe quickly became Morris Gershvin and after the first few years at his leather trade, set out to be an entrepreneur in this land of opportunity. Always skirting disaster, always bobbing up again in some other business, his optimism never failed. His daughter remembered him years later as not hard enough for business success.

"He wouldn't use the car horn at a cyclist in front of us lest he startle him," recalled Frances Gershwin Godowsky, "and he always gave to panhandlers for fear of missing someone who really needed aid."

Rose was made of sterner stuff, handling the family finances and keeping the family disaster insurance, a diamond ring which went in and out of the pawnshop as the family's fortunes rose and fell. Morris Gershvin's ventures into hotels, restaurants,

Left: Morris and Rose Gershvin (as he spelled it then) in a studio portrait the year of their wedding, 1895. Below: Ira at about eleven with his pet dog. Bottom, George's painting of his mother. Done in the 1930's, it shows her as she would have looked at about 1914, capturing the essence of her regal personality. Rose was always a stylish dresser, as even her 1895 photo shows, who not only wore fashionable clothes well but could design them herself. She also loved the theater and later traveled with Frances when her daughter appeared as a child dancer.

Gershwin knew only his maternal grandparents, who emigrated to the United States from Russia with daughter Rose about 1892. Right, the sketch he made of his grandmother Bruskin in 1929. Below, left, the painting he did of Grandfather Bruskin, shown as a younger man earlier in the century, in dark clothes and hat, with carefully placed elements of drapery and New York buildings suggesting the move from Russia to a new world. Right, below, Rose Gershwin at sixteen, about the time of her arrival here. Elegantly coiffed and dressed, she wears the jewelry that emphasizes the family's status.

Russian and Turkish baths, bakeries, a cigar store and pool parlor—he once even tried bookmaking, as he and Rose liked going to the race tracks whenever money was good—were typical of the times. In the expansive America of that era, Morris might be no tycoon but there was space enough for his optimistic independence.

A handsome girl, Rose Gershvin carried a regal air in later life, aided by an innate sense of style. "She ought to have been the business person," according to daughter Frances, "but that wasn't the way things went in proper families. She could design, too—hats, dresses."

Rose ran the family life, but she was no cliché "Jewish mother." George and Ira roamed the city freely—New York was considered safe enough—and she doesn't seem to have been disturbed by George's boyish sins. These arose chiefly from school, which did not suit George's restlessly physical personality. Public schools then followed strict disciplinary routines, not to speak of requiring much book study, and all he wanted was to be out playing the street games at which he was a neighborhood champion, or roaming the city with Ira.

Although the schools also tried to inculcate musical culture, George turned up his boyish nose at such sissy ideas. Yet he could be fascinated by something heard on the wing, and his forays into the then-downtown black section brought to his ears the ragtime and jazz of café musicians rehearsing. To that music he did pay attention.

TOWARD MUSIC

The Gershvin family life had few ties to the past. All New York used to change apartments every October, when the customary yearly leases expired, but the Gershvins did it even more often, as some 28 moves occurred during George's first eighteen years! Names were treated casually. Although "Jacob" on his birth certificate, George was never called that. Ira was called "Izzy" and supposed his name to be Isadore until he was 32 and got his first

George Gershwin was only fifteen when he went to work as a pianist "song plugger" at Jerome Remick, a leading popular song publisher in a whole new American musical genre. An instant success, despite his youth, as a demonstrator, George had this man-of-the-world studio portrait made of himself about 1914.

Every music publisher on "Tin Pan Alley" employed a group of song pluggers, who also often traveled on business. George met many leading stage personalities, for whom he accompanied as well, as he did later on tours with Louise Dresser and Nora Bayes.

passport, when he discovered his birth certificate said "Israel". The last name, already altered by Morris, was changed later by George to "Gershwin," and the whole family followed suit.

Religion was equally casual—Ira had a bar mitzvah, but not George or Arthur. Friday night poker games were a family fixture, and Rose enjoyed the backstage friendship of actresses at the flourishing Yiddish theaters. Morris sometimes went to the opera. In sum, the immigrant family plunged into New York life without a backward glance.

Rose particularly kept a sharp eye on American standards. Ira, the intellectual son, had been admitted to Townsend Harris High School for bright boys, and when Rose discovered that a piano was a fixture in every proper American home, in one came for Ira. Happily for word-oriented Ira, it was George who at once sat down and played.

Apparently unknown to his family, he had been teaching himself on a friend's piano after being literally seized by the musical bug through the playing of a talented schoolmate. Maxie Rosenzweig, later the famed violinist Max Rosen, played for school recitals, and George discovered music. Typically, he hadn't asked for lessons, but learned the piano by ear. However, his mother at once started him with one of those neighborhood lady teachers who then proliferated all over America.

He also began to attend concerts, keeping a scrapbook of programs and information on musicians, so we know that in 1912 and 1913 he heard Leo Ornstein, Efrem Zimbalist, Josef Lhevinne and Leopold Godowsky. He played piano with the Beethoven Society Orchestra, a determinedly classical community group using P.S. 63 for its performances. It was another member who introduced him to his first really good teacher, Charles Hambitzer.

Hambitzer was a classically trained composer and pianist who was a well-known soloist with orchestras and ensembles of the day. Upon hearing young George play his *pièce de resistance,* the "William Tell" Overture, Hambitzer commented about the previous teacher, "Let's shoot Goldfarb and not with an apple on his head, either."

However, he took George as a pupil without fee and was soon writing to a relative: "A pupil who will

Among the newly risen popular song composers, Irving Berlin, shown left in a later photo, stood out after his "Alexander's Ragtime Band" in 1911. The rhythms of ragtime and jazz expressed rapid social changes, bringing in such innovations as women's gymnastics, shown below in a 1904 photograph at Teachers' College. Bottom, a candid shot of Gershwin composing at T. B. Harms. In 1917 he left Remick to become a composer, and went on Harms' payroll for $35 a week as a staff composer. He also entered the Broadway stage world by becoming a rehearsal pianist for shows.

make his mark in music if anybody will. The boy is a genius, without doubt; he's just crazy about music and can't wait until it's time to take his lessons. No watching the clock for this boy. He wants to go in for this modern stuff, jazz and whatnot. But I'm not going to let him for a while. I'll see that he gets a firm foundation in the standard music first."

It was an astonishing statement about a boy of fourteen who only a few years before had seemingly had no interest in music, but Hambitzer was right. Gershwin's pattern was set for lifelong total absorption in music. Also interesting is Hambitzer's attitude that "jazz" was a respectable part of "modern stuff," by which he probably meant Arnold Schoenberg and Igor Stravinsky. Apparently, Hambitzer wasn't opposed to new trends, as were so many other serious musicians. He simply felt that a student should be well-grounded before breaking the mold. That teacher and student were sympathetic is evident from Gershwin's own comment in later years that he revered Hambitzer's memory.

Under his guidance, the youngster progressed

rapidly. By the next year he had written a couple of songs, been the pianist for a summer resort and on May 1, 1914, first appeared in public as composer and pianist, playing a tango he had written, at a concert of a club brother Ira belonged to.

Today, we would ask why he didn't go to a conservatory. At that time, such a route didn't inevitably suggest itself. Conservatories were "European," and an all-American boy often preferred private teachers. He also often did what George did next—shake off school after graduation from the elementary grades. Although mother Rose put George into commercial high school with the safe career of accountancy in mind, George stuck it out for only a year. He informed his family that through a friend he had found a job as pianist at Jerome Remick, a leading popular music publisher.

Although only 15, he was strong-willed like his mother, so he won the argument with her and went off to earn $15 a week, a not inconsiderable sum for a boy then. He was the youngest "song plugger" ever hired in Tin Pan Alley.

Influenced by David Belasco and audiences' love of spectacle, theater production all through Gershwin's youth remained highly elaborate. Opposite page, top, the first act setting of Richard Mansfield's "Cyrano de Bergerac," 1898, called for a seventeenth-century Parisian "hotel de ville," used in that century as a theater. The scene shows Mansfield, front with sword, in the climactic duel episode. This page, a Victorian English country mansion drawing room was created for the first act of "The Liars," by the famous English playwright, Henry Arthur Jones, in 1898. The characters shown were played, left to right, by Blanche Burton, John Drew

(leading star of the day and uncle of the yet-unknown John, Lionel and Ethel Barrymore), Isabelle Irving and Arthur Byron. Byron remained a leading stage and later screen actor for many years.

Meanwhile, mechanical entertainment devices were appearing. Facing page, bottom, shows Broadway, looking up from Herald Square to the then-new Times Tower looming at Forty-Second Street, about 1909. Prominent in the scene is a huge sign advertising the Edison home phonograph. By that year, his kinetescope had evolved into two-reel motion pictures, shown in storefront theaters for a nickel a ticket.

From pre-World War I days to post-War, the theater changed. In 1898, audiences were thrilled by the melodrama of "Way Down East," shown below in the climactic scene when the heroine accuses her seducer. But in 1918, even a musical could be a comedy about women in politics. Bottom: a scene from "Ladies First," in which star Nora Bayes flirtatiously pours coffee for Irving Fisher. Gershwin got two songs interpolated into this show. Also American in theme were the musicals of George M. Cohan, whose wife, Ethel Levey, right, was his leading lady.

TOWARD COMPOSING

Female singing stars appeared in vaudeville, solo recitals and musical comedy. They came constantly to Remick and other publishers, seeking new songs, and met the youthful composer, George Gershwin. His first published song was accepted because Sophie Tucker liked it. Below, Nora Bayes in costume for one of her solo appearances. Gershwin's contact with her went beyond interpolations in her 1918 show. He traveled with her as accompanist on a tour and resisted the imperious Miss Bayes' demand that he change one of his songs to suit her ideas of her style.

Tin Pan Alley—the words evoke a long-vanished world, a row of music publishers along West 28th Street from whose windows in summer could be heard pianos which probably gave the row its name. Songs and light piano pieces flowed from Tin Pan Alley by the hundreds to supply American households entertaining themselves by singing and playing. Vaudeville and stage musicals needed songs. Stars such as Eva Tanguay, Elsie Janis, Ethel Levey and Nora Bayes came daily seeking new hits for themselves. The song plugger's job was to play for them in the hope they would sing the songs on stage, record them and set America to buying sheet music and records.

George loved it all, not least because he was soon regarded as the best pianist at Remick. He was quick to style a song for a particular performer, as his improvisational ability was phenomenal. He also wrote songs steadily and often performed them for clients. Among those he impressed were the teenage vaudeville dancing stars, Fred and Adele Astaire. Once George said he'd like to do a show for them some day, and they laughingly agreed. No one had done any such thing for them, yet in less than ten years it was to happen.

Although Remick refused to publish any of his songs, George's writing gradually made him realize that the average Tin Pan Alley song, written for a mass audience with slight playing and singing abilities, couldn't compare with music written for Broadway. Jerome Kern particularly caught his ear. Like Kern and other unknown young composers, George hoped to get a song "interpolated" into a show.

This custom had arisen from the appearance of vaudeville stars in musical comedy. Although a composer wrote the musical, the star's audience expected to see him or her perform the kind of specialty for which the star was known. When this special song was sung, the show stopped dead, for the "star turn" didn't even have to relate to the musical as a whole! Naturally, this custom destroyed the integrity of musicals, and operetta composers, such as Victor Herbert, often didn't allow it, but interpolations provided a way for new talent to break in.

In 1919, George's first big song hit became a signature song for star Al Jolson, shown below on the cover of the sheet music for "Swanee." Bottom, Gershwin's close friend, lyricist Irving Caesar, who wrote the words to his music in a single evening's inspired collaboration.

One or two successes with interpolations were enough to make young Gershwin break with Tin Pan Alley. In 1917 he left Remick to become a rehearsal pianist for Broadway shows. When star Vivienne Segal sang two of his songs, he was at last published for the first time—and by Remick.

Although World War I now hovered over boys of George's and Ira's age, it passed him by. Much more important to him was Max Dreyfus, head of T. B. Harms, another famous music publisher. Dreyfus put him on the Harms payroll, just to compose. Super-star Nora Bayes chose his "Some Wonderful Sort of Someone" to interpolate in her political musical, "Ladies First." Then she added "The Real American Folk Song (Is a Rag)", with lyrics by Arthur Francis. This *nom de plume* veiled Ira, who had begun writing lyrics for other song writers, and didn't want to trade on George's reputation. Despite modest accomplishments, George was a comer.

More than obvious talent caused theater people to believe in the young Gershwin. He had enormous charm, compounded of a highly sociable personality, an easy way of making friends, and a belief in himself so sincere that everyone else believed in him, too. In 1919, when Alex A. Aarons wanted to start producing shows, he chose the twenty-one-year-old Gershwin to write a complete musical.

A modest success, "La, La, Lucile" signaled that something new was on the way. In contrast to the sentimental or trivial musicals still dominating the stage, it was a sophisticated farce about divorce. It delighted Aarons, who with his later partner, Vinton Freedley, was to produce Gershwin musicals until 1933.

At the same time, George was working privately on more ambitious forms, such as a movement for string quartet he called "Lullaby," and which he later used in his first attempt with opera. He was now seriously set on being a composer, as Charles Hambitzer had died in 1918, taking with him the idea of a concert pianist's career.

However, all his life Gershwin played the piano constantly. It was his way of composing, since from his constant improvising his ideas arose. His musical memory was such that he could hold in mind an impressive amount of original material. In later life he once lost a notebook filled with notes for compositions, and when his brother Ira lamented the loss, George shrugged it off. "There's plenty more where they came from." At his death he had apparently composed an entire string quartet, as his friend Merle Armitage heard him play a good deal of it, but he hadn't yet had time to write it down, so it was lost.

With his first musical on the stage, George casually tossed off a rollicking ditty with Irving Caesar as lyricist in an hour one evening at the Gershwin family apartment. "Swanee" was picked up by Al Jolson, a vastly popular entertainer, as an interpolation in his current show, "Sinbad." It became a signature song for Jolson and so popular that it brought Gershwin $10,000 a year, then a large sum. It was the single biggest hit of his lifetime, although not at all typical of the Gershwin style as later developed. Even four years later, on his first visit to England, a customs official checking his passport, asked "George Gershwin, the writer of 'Swanee'?"

However trivial, "Swanee" catapulted George into the show business-literary-artistic circles of New York. As the Twenties opened, Greenwich Village was the center, where Lou Paley, a sometime lyricist for George, lived with his wife, Emily, whose sister Leonore would later marry Ira Gershwin. S. N. Behrman, the playwright, Groucho Marx, Irving Caesar, B. G. DeSylva (another Gershwin lyricist, but later famous as one of the song-writing trio of DeSylva, Brown and Henderson) and Howard Dietz, lyricist for Arthur Schwartz, gathered there.

In 1921 George met Jules Glaenzer, head of Cartier, the jewelers, and entered the East Side uptown world of international celebrities. The famous Glaenzer parties would include Douglas Fairbanks, Jack Dempsey, Charles Chaplin, Noel Coward, Lord and Lady Louis Mountbatten, Fanny Brice, Maurice Chevalier, Gertrude Lawrence, the Astaires—the list was endless. Into this world George slipped as easily as into the Greenwich Village circle.

At all parties, Gershwin played the piano, not because he had to but because he wanted to. George S. Kaufman, the witty playwright, once said that peo-

---

Above, the letter George wrote home from England in 1923 about his recognition by a customs official as the composer of "Swanee." Below, the house on 103rd Street, New York, with today's identifying plaque, inset, where all the Gershwins lived after 1925. The house became an effervescent center for all of George's and Ira's many friends.

ple had heard all of George's new music for a show so often that on opening night they thought they were attending a revival. He simply couldn't help playing, and everyone who heard him testified that he played as no one else could or did.

It is remarkable that no one who ever knew him has had a bad word to say of him, not even women, although he was certainly what was then called a "ladies' man" and today a "womanizer." Although he often talked about marrying, he never did. His absolute concentration on music, and perhaps his close family ties seemed to prevent his marrying. Rosamund Walling, one of the only two women he is known to have come close to marrying, said shrewdly, "He never made me feel needed." Yet she remembered him with the same affectionate glow as everyone else felt.

And then, after all, he had Ira, so different in his retiring, intellectual, easy-going ways. By 1921 Ira had made his own Broadway success, as lyricist with Vincent Youmans as composer for "Two Little Girls In Blue." Still using the name of Arthur Francis, he collaborated only on and off with George until 1924, when he also began to use his own name.

With Ira as the perfect partner, the family circle was complete. Whether in the five-story house on 103rd Street, or on Riverside Drive or on East 72nd Street, they all lived together or near by, a houseful of mama, papa, Ira and Leonore, sister Frances, and always a dozen or more friends in and out at all hours. The easy morals of the Twenties made girl friends no problem to a man as attractive as Gershwin.

FIRST TRY WITH OPERA

After "La, La, Lucile" and "Swanee," Gershwin was able to get from producer George White, formerly a dancer in a show for which George had been rehearsal pianist, a commitment to do the music for the second edition of "George White's Scandals." This series of annual revues had been begun by White in hopes of rivaling the Ziegfeld Follies. They never really did so, but Gershwin wrote for five of them, and some classic Gershwin songs resulted— "Stairway to Paradise" and "Somebody Loves Me," for example.

Most interesting, however, is the one-act opera George wrote for the 1922 "Scandals." Called "Blue Monday," to a libretto by B. G. DeSylva, who suggested the idea, it concerned black life in Harlem, that milieu which had fascinated Gershwin since childhood. Unfortunately, it was performed by white entertainers in blackface, quite a common custom at the time. As such performances were always comedic, reviewers naturally thought the little

Below, original score page for "Blue Monday," Gershwin's first attempt at an opera, done for the 1922 George White's "Scandals." Bottom, George, with pipe, and Alex Aarons, producer of "La, La, Lucile," his first musical comedy, which marked Gershwin as a bright new talent.

tragedy was a comedy gone wrong. They blasted it, and George White dropped it after one performance.

However, the orchestra for that "Scandals" was led by Paul Whiteman, whose group also headlined at a dance palace called the Palais Royal. A classically trained musician, Whiteman was so impressed with "Blue Monday" that he later gave concert performances of the work under a new title, "135th Street." The original work was orchestrated by Will Vodery, a black musician who had aided a younger, out-of-work Gershwin, an example of his ability to make friends even among unlikely groups such as blacks. The later "135th Street" concert version was orchestrated by Whiteman's arranger, Ferde Grofé, who was to play an even more important role in Gershwin's career.

Meanwhile, George put the "Blue Monday" fiasco behind him, as he was to do all his life with failures. He had too many new songs pouring out to brood over the past, and besides writing the annual "Scandals" shows, he continued to get songs into other people's shows. He co-authored one musical, "Our Nell," with a composer named William Daly, who soon became a close friend. An academically trained musician, Daly gave Gershwin expert advice on his concert compositions, was his favorite arranger for shows and often his conductor.

Besides working privately on serious composition, Gershwin took periodic instruction from several notable teachers. His ambivalent attitude toward formal instruction was typically American. One moment he could do it all himself—hadn't he first played the piano by ear and absorbed all kinds of musical influences on his own? Then he would find a technical barrier to what he wanted to express, so he would be off to sit at the feet of a master. All his teachers were the best—Artur Bodansky, Edward Kilenyi, Henry Cowell, Wallingford Riegger, Joseph Schillinger—but with all of them study was sporadic. A stern formalist like Rubin Goldmark, although head of the composition department at Juilliard School of Music and a teacher of Aaron Copland, got nowhere with Gershwin. He made the mistake of saying that Gershwin had learned a great deal from him when Gershwin showed him his "Lullaby," actually written several years before. That finished the lessons, confirming

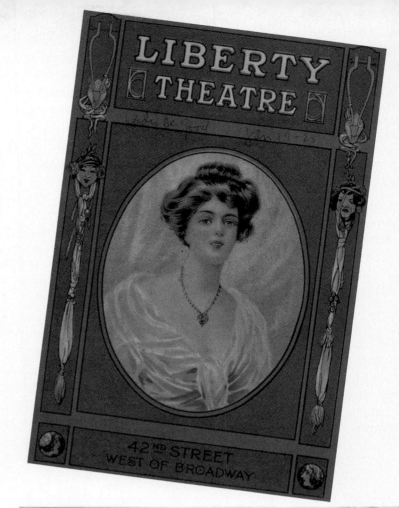

Theater programs in the 1920's often had colorful covers especially designed for each theater, as shown above right. George's show, "Lady, Be Good!" ran in 1924-25 at the Liberty, still on Forty-Second Street, New York. Below, Ann Pennington, dancing star of George White's annual "Scandals" shows, for which George composed. He did five of them, all told.

As his fame grew, George Gershwin became one of the most photographed, sketched and caricatured men of his time. Below, Churchill Ettinger's portrait, drawn in typically 1920's angular modern style, complete with George's ever-present cigar. Bottom, Alfred Frueh's caricature of singer Eva Gauthier and Gershwin at the piano, done for a magazine at the time of their 1923 recital. Although still at the beginning, when compared with his later career, Gershwin was already widely known in theatrical and musical circles as a song composer and as a pianist of extraordinary talent.

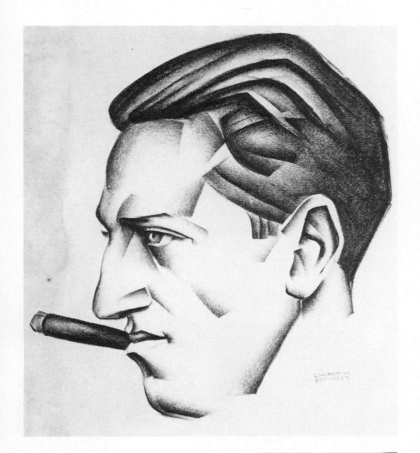

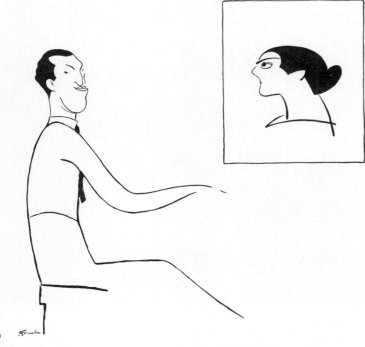

George's impatience with teachers—until the next felt need came along.

Altogether, it's impossible to say how much formal music Gershwin "knew" as he approached 1924, which would be the watershed year of his career. In December, 1923, he did a concert with the recital singer Eva Gauthier, who was a champion of "modern" music. This term then embraced everything from "jazz," understood to mean black music brought from New Orleans and Memphis, to such composers as Ravel and Stravinsky. Gauthier wanted to mount a song concert which would include Baroque composers Byrd and Purcell, moderns Schoenberg, Bartok, Milhaud and Hindemith, and most daringly, American song writers such as Irving Berlin, Jerome Kern and George Gershwin. George, of course, was also a pianist able to accompany her in the entire American group.

Such a mixed program sounds bizarre today, but Gauthier was striking a blow in a musical war. The turmoil in American musical life involved furious disputes over "modern" music vs. the lingering influence of nineteenth-century romanticism, equally emotional debates over European influence vs. "native" American music, and even racism and anti-Semitism, all resulting in a boiling stew. The virulence of the musical wars then fought seems almost unbelievable today, but must be understood. The turmoil was the background for George Gershwin's stature in his time and for the uproar one composition could cause.

Gauthier's concert, celebrated as it was, soon was eclipsed by an even more famous event in February, 1924. Paul Whiteman, as a classically trained musician who had succeeded in jazz-influenced popular music, was naturally interested in the raging musical fights over "jazz." The success of Gauthier's recital at highly respectable Aeolian Hall gave him the idea of creating a "jazz" concert there. He would also go Gauthier one better; he would have original compositions on the program. He asked Victor Herbert, a veritable icon of the musical establishment, and he asked George Gershwin, whose "Blue Monday" he remembered vividly.

The story is well known—how Gershwin blithely agreed (any American boy can do it)—how he found out in a newspaper item on January 4 that the

An Experiment
in
MODERN MUSIC

AEOLIAN HALL

1924

February
12

Paul Whiteman made careful preparations for his innovative "jazz" concert at Aeolian Hall, even to an elaborate program cover design, left, in purple and gold. Below, the program, showing Zez Confrey's segment in the first half, the "Suite of Serenades" composed by Victor Herbert for the second half, and the almost-last position of "Rhapsody in Blue." Herbert was asked to show that his mainstream nineteenth century style could take on a jazz hue, and he did so rather successfully. However, he could offer little beyond the interesting color lent his serenades by his use of jazz instruments.

PROGRAM

First Half

1. TRUE FORM OF JAZZ
   a. Ten Years Ago—"Livery Stable Blues".................*LaRocca*
   b. With Modern Embellishment—"Mama Loves Papa".................*Baer*

2. COMEDY SELECTIONS
   a. Origin of "Yes, We Have No Bananas".................*Silver*
   b. Instrumental Comedy—"So This Is Venice".................*Thomas*
   (Featuring Ross Gorman) (Adapted from "The Carnival of Venice")

3. CONTRAST—LEGITIMATE SCORING VS. JAZZING
   a. Selection in True Form—"Whispering".................*Schonberger*
   b. Same Selection with Jazz Treatment

4. RECENT COMPOSITIONS WITH MODERN SCORE
   a. "Limehouse Blues".................*Braham*
   b. "I Love You".................*Archer*
   c. "Raggedy Ann".................*Kern*

5. ZEZ CONFREY (Piano)
   a. Medley Popular Airs
   b. "Kitten on the Keys".................*Confrey*
   c. "Ice Cream and Art"
   d. "Nickel in the Slot".................*Confrey*
      Accompanied by the Orchestra

6. FLAVORING A SELECTION WITH BORROWED THEMES
   "Russian Rose".................*Grofé*
   (Based on "The Volga Boat Song")

(Program continued)

7. SEMI SYMPHONIC ARRANGEMENT OF POPULAR MELODIES
   Consisting of
   "Alexander's Ragtime Band".................⎞
   "A Pretty Girl is Like a Melody".................⎬ *Berlin*
   "Orange Blossoms in California".................⎠

Second Half

8. A SUITE OF SERENADES.................*Herbert*
   a. Spanish
   b. Chinese
   c. Cuban
   d. Oriental

9. ADAPTATION OF STANDARD SELECTIONS TO DANCE RHYTHM
   a. "Pale Moon".................*Logan*
   b. "To a Wild Rose".................*McDowell*
   c. "Chansonette".................*Friml*

10. GEORGE GERSHWIN (Piano)
    "A Rhapsody in Blue".................*Gershwin*
    Accompanied by the Orchestra

11. IN THE FIELD OF CLASSICS
    "Pomp and Circumstance".................*Elgar*

Chickering Piano Used.

20

The composer of "Rhapsody in Blue" became instantly world famous. Below, even his hands, playing a crossover passage in the "Rhapsody," were photographed, while the sketch, right, by Lupas, probably from a photograph, shows him about 1925. Bottom, conferring on the 1925 concert performance of his earlier short opera, "Blue Monday," re-titled "135th Street," left to right, arranger Ferde Grofé, critic-composer Deems Taylor, Paul Whiteman, singer Blossom Seeley, and Gershwin. Paul Whiteman was always to believe in the one-act opera, giving it yet another performance in 1936, with new orchestration by Grofé.

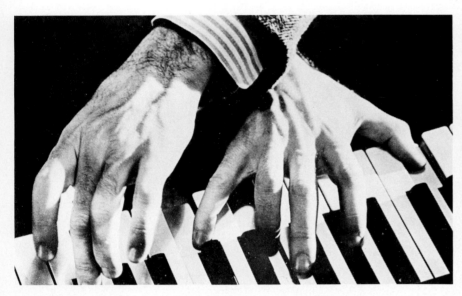

concert was to be on February 11 (he had only a few sketches on paper)—and how he managed to get it done as a two-piano piece by January 25, with Ferde Grofé frantically orchestrating the piece up until February 4. The piano solo part never did get entirely written in time, but that was no problem— George was playing it and he could improvise in masterly fashion.

Whiteman had seen to it that the audience was packed with big names: Leopold Godowsky, Fritz Kreisler, Sergei Rachmaninoff, Walter Damrosch, Jascha Heifetz and Leopold Stokowsky are just samples. Otto Kahn, who practically supported the Metropolitan Opera, and George's friend, Jules Glaenzer, stood as sponsors. But the program was actually trivial for such a sophisticated audience. Even a group of "Serenades," written for the occasion by Victor Herbert, using jazz band instrumentation, seemed tame, and they were soon bored.

For the next to the last number, George Gershwin came out to the piano, clarinetist Ross Gorman lifted his instrument, and for the first time anywhere the thrilling clarinet glissando wail opened "Rhapsody in Blue." Suddenly, the audience was transfixed. At the end, the hall exploded. Here it was, an authentic American voice in an unforgettable concert piece. Its color, call it jazz or what you will, so stamped itself on music that everything afterward with anything like the same color has tended to sound like Gershwin.

Not that "Rhapsody in Blue" settled the then-raging debate over "modernism." Critic Lawrence Gilman fumed: "Lifeless melody, derivative, stale and inexpressive." However, Olin Downes of "The New York Times" cautiously approved. Such split critical reaction was to greet Gershwin's serious work to the end.

However, in democratic American fashion, he cared most about the ecstatic public acceptance. In the next ten years, "Rhapsody in Blue" was performed so often as to earn him a quarter of a million dollars, an enormous sum for a "serious" work. It became so identified with him that at his death, even after all the other works he had composed, headlines said that the composer of "Rhapsody in Blue" had died.

Gershwin's creative life in the theater bloomed in the later 1920's with a series of musicals that explored a variety of styles. The first, "Lady, Be Good!," opening in late 1924, gave Fred and Adele Astaire their first major Broadway success. They had been a brother-and-sister dance act in vaudeville since childhood, and met George Gershwin as an equally youthful "song plugger" at Remick. Their previous attempts to invade Broadway had been only mildly successful before this show, in a scene from which they are shown below, demonstrating their distinctive dance style.

Gershwin himself reacted to the stunning success of the Whiteman concert chiefly with satisfaction at having "crossed over," demonstrating that "popular" and "serious" music could blend. He had no time to imagine the future success of the "Rhapsody," since he had three shows to write that same year. In addition to another edition of George White's "Scandals," there was "Primrose," a musical he did in London, this time with Ira along to collaborate on the lyrics, and under his own name at last. The third musical, in December, fulfilled that youthful wish made with Fred and Adele Astaire. It was "Lady, Be Good!" and it made the brother-sister team into major Broadway stars while confirming that George and Ira Gershwin were first-rank creative talents in the musical theater.

All this work didn't overburden Gershwin. Where Ira was a typical writer, always delaying actual work, always rewriting, George composed fluently and constantly. He didn't always even record what he had composed, and his notebooks are full of phrases and bars, reminders of what he thought was good. But when he had finished something he believed in, he never gave up on it.

Although still working on such old-fashioned collaborative musicals as the operetta, "Song of the Flame," and pulling songs out of shows if they didn't seem to work, Gershwin tried to place "The Man I Love" into no less than three of his musicals. He would have tried a fourth time, but Lady Louis Mountbatten, on hearing it in "Lady, Be Good!" before the song was pulled out, asked to take the unused sheet music with her back to London. She gave it to her favorite club orchestra, and "The Man I Love" became a London hit. Not until a few years later when singer Helen Morgan took it up and made the song her signature number, did it become a New York success. It remains the only Gershwin classic which never appeared in a show.

The Broadway musical stage was changing, but the 1920s saw a bewildering mix of newly sophisticated composing such as that of Gershwin and Jerome Kern with European-style operettas by Sigmund Romberg and simplistic song writing of the Tin Pan Alley level. In his satire on Tin Pan Alley,

Far left, Helen Morgan, great café singer of the 1920's, made "The Man I Love" her signature song, after Gershwin couldn't find a suitable place for it in three successive musicals. Near left, Lady Louis (Edwina) Mountbatten, who had previously made the song a London and Paris hit by taking it back with her from New York and giving it to her favorite club orchestra. Bottom, George Gershwin's piano, as it stands today in the apartment of Mrs. Judy Gershwin, widow of Arthur, the youngest Gershwin son. Both his and George's music appear on the piano rack.

With Ira as his lyricist, George Gershwin hit his theater stride. In 1926 he created "Oh, Kay!" for Gertrude Lawrence, shown right in the famous scene where she sang "Someone to Watch Over Me" to a rag doll. The very next year George and Ira repeated for Fred and Adele Astaire with a second musical, "Funny Face." Below, Fred Astaire posed with his ingenue lead, Gertrude MacDonald. Exactly thirty years later, with a new story, "Funny Face" became an Astaire film, bottom, with Audrey Hepburn, center, as his leading lady, and sophisticated comedienne Kay Thompson.

William Merritt Daly, below, a university-educated musician with an easy-going personality, early became closest to Gershwin, as collaborator and friend, after his brother Ira. Daly's untimely death in 1936 devastated Gershwin. Bottom, a scene from Gershwin's "Tip-Toes" of 1925 shows, left to right, Andrew Toombes, dancing star Queenie Smith and Harry Watson Jr. as stranded vaudevillians. The cast included a very young Jeannette MacDonald, later to be an important star of film musicals. "Tip-Toes" was George and Ira's second collaboration entirely with each other.

"June Moon," the playwright Ring Lardner included a scene where a group of effervescent song writers is silenced by the news "Gershwin is in the building!" One by one they slip out to get a glimpse of him, although he never appears in the scene.

Yet Gershwin continued to be a down-to-earth workman. Accepting the musical stage conventions of the time, he adapted cheerfully to their demands, even when friends pointed out he was wasting his music on trivial plots. The fact accounts for the death of Gershwin shows even while the music lives perhaps more strongly today than when it first was heard.

While collaborating on "Song of the Flame" with Herbert Stothart and writing the score of "Tip-Toes" for dancing star Queenie Smith, Gershwin was composing a concerto for the New York Symphony, whose conductor, Walter Damrosch, signed him to a seven-performance contract before the piece was written. The uproar in the musical world had continued over the place of jazz—and of George Gershwin—in serious American composing, and Damrosch was on Gershwin's side.

In a typical comment, George said he signed the contract and then bought a book to find out what a concerto was—a bit of American-style swagger. Actually, he bought around this time a well-known standard text on orchestration. He had quickly learned from critical comments after "Rhapsody in Blue" that the Broadway practice of the orchestrator being someone other than the composer wouldn't do in concert music, and he was determined to orchestrate the concerto. In fact, all his subsequent scores are entirely in his own hand.

Not that he didn't take suggestions. As a theater man, he was quite accustomed to taking ideas—the "Rhapsody in Blue" clarinet glissando, for example, was apparently performed that way at a rehearsal by the player and retained by a delighted Gershwin. He trusted Bill Daly's suggestions so completely that Daly once had to deny in print that he was really the composer of Gershwin's works. Nor did he hear his work orchestrally in his mind. He composed the Concerto in F on two pianos, with Daly on the second one and hired a 60-piece orches-

THE
THREE K's

tra for a private run-through, with Daly conducting, for Walter Damrosch.

Gershwin's ability to work on several projects at once can be seen in late 1925. With "Tip-Toes" and "Song of the Flame" both still in production, Gershwin performed the Concerto in F on December 3 at Carnegie Hall with the New York Symphony Orchestra conducted by Walter Damrosch.

The concerto created the same audience impact as had the "Rhapsody in Blue" and the same divided critical reception. "Of all those writing the music of today . . . he alone actually expresses us," wrote critic Samuel Chotzinoff, who had also enthusiastically greeted the "Rhapsody," while Lawrence Gilman was again hostile and Olin Downes remained cautiously supportive.

George also began writing piano solos around this time, although his schedule of theater work prevented his finishing more than the five now known as the "Preludes for Piano." His social life, whether he was in New York or London, was also very active. He loved parties as much as his brother Ira avoided them.

Work, however, was always the greatest pleasure, and now a new star awaited his touch, Gertrude Lawrence, the English actress-singer who had made a New York hit in "Charlot's Revue" of 1924. Right alongside his composing and performing the piano preludes, Gershwin in 1926 created "Oh, Kay!" for the incomparable Miss Lawrence, whose singing of "Someone to Watch Over Me" to a rag doll has remained a memorable theater moment.

The 246-performance success of "Oh, Kay!" confirmed the position of George and Ira Gershwin at the top of those writing for the musical stage of the 1920's, since their bright, unsentimental, even satirical style brought a new era to Broadway.

CAREER CROWN

The five years from 1926 through 1932 represent a crest in Gershwin's career. In both the popular and serious music worlds he was the most famous composer alive, although his concert productions amounted only to the "Rhapsody in Blue," the "Concerto in F," the "Five Piano Preludes" and the tone poem, "An American in Paris," which he produced in 1928 for Walter Damrosch and the New York Philharmonic, an orchestra recently formed by merging Damrosch's New York Symphony and the Philharmonic Orchestra.

Yet this small output produced an impact far out of proportion to its size. Each new creation was greeted, reviewed, and furiously debated with enough attention for the entire body of work of an-

Below, the still-young "Time" magazine featured Gershwin on its cover of July 20, 1925 as a newsmaking composer. Bottom, Ira Gershwin, with Leonore Strunsky, left, whom he married in 1926, and her sister, Emily Paley, of whom George was particularly fond. Hers was the first portrait he painted when he began with oils.

FIFTEEN CENTS

TIME
The Weekly News-Magazine

GEORGE GERSHWIN
He rhapsodizes blues
(See Page 14)

VOL. VI. No. 3   JULY 20, 1925

other composer. Even before "An American in Paris" had its first performance in December, 1928, its coming had been heralded since March of that year.

Gershwin also increased his standing as a concert performer after the series as soloist in his "Concerto in F." He began appearing at the huge summer outdoor concerts then a New York fixture at the Lewisohn Stadium in upper Manhattan, first as pianist, then as conductor in 1929, directing his "An American in Paris."

His approach to conducting followed his typically American "hands-on" spirit. Delightedly accepting the idea of conducting, he practised with records, his teacher of the moment, Edward Kilenyi, and even in front of a mirror. Not only did he succeed with a symphony orchestra, but at opening nights of his new shows.

And the shows came fast and furious, each one quite different from the last. The series of these years, begun with the success of "Oh, Kay!," now continued with "Strike Up the Band" in 1927. It failed "out of town," as they said then about any performances away from New York. The satirical anti-war "book" (as the plot of a musical was called) by the cynically witty George S. Kaufman, attracted the critics but not audiences immersed in the apparently endless prosperity of the "Golden Twenties."

As always, Gershwin quickly went on to another show, a more acceptably frothy "Funny Face" the same year, in which Fred and Adele Astaire starred for 244 performances. Only two months after its November opening, he was again collaborating, this time on another of the operetta-type musicals which weren't really his metier. Yet "Rosalie," tailored for Marilyn Miller, perhaps the brightest star of the day in the musical theater, was an even bigger hit than "Funny Face," to judge by 335 performances.

In 1928, even while taking a three-month European trip which was like a triumphal progress through London, Paris and Vienna, and finishing "An American in Paris," Gershwin produced a new musical for Gertrude Lawrence, "Treasure Girl," whose poorly conceived book doomed it, began writing "East is West" for Florenz Ziegfeld, then laid that aside when Ziegfeld decided to go for another idea, which became "Show Girl."

Program cover, above, for the theater where Florenz Ziegfeld presented his shows. Here, "Rosalie," co-composed by Gershwin with Sigmund Romberg, had its long run. Below, George with Ernest Hutcheson, leading pianist of the day, who offered him a composing refuge in 1925 at Chatauqua, New York, where Hutcheson coached advanced students.

Another of Gershwin's country refuges was the farm of James Warburg and his wife, composer Kay Swift, in upstate New York, where George is shown, below, in 1927. He and Ira emerged with the score for "Strike Up The Band." Bottom, Marilyn Miller making an entrance in "Rosalie," described with humorous affection by critic Alexander Woollcott as a matter of fifty girls in "simple peasant costumes of satin and chiffon," all squealing, "Here she comes!" and 'hussars kneeling "to express an emotion too strong for words," after which "on walks Marilyn Miller." She was Ziegfeld's brightest star.

Gershwin even found time for an entirely new interest. After acquiring a Riverside Drive penthouse apartment, whose Art Deco furnishings promptly were photographed for a magazine, he began collecting art. His cousin, Henry Botkin, a professional painter, had remarked that the walls needed something to decorate them, a remark which was enough to start George off with his usual enthusiasm.

In art, as in music, Gershwin's tastes belonged to his time, and he acquired, largely through Botkin's anonymous buying, at modest prices, a number of modernists. The collection, finally of some 144 items, became highly valuable in later years. As Botkin had also suggested that one became a better collector if one tried one's own hand, George just as promptly turned a longtime casual interest in sketching into a fullblown avocation in oil painting. With no more aid than his astonished cousin's guidance, he developed rapidly into a respectable painter. Although his taste in collecting included the abstractionists, he did not make the amateur's mistake of imitating. His own interest was in character, and he went straight for representational portraiture.

He became as devoted to painting as to composing, often giving late night hours to it, then propping the unfinished work at the foot of his bed so he would see it on waking and bring fresh ideas to it. He said he regarded painting as simply another expression of the same creative impulse that made him compose. He was probably right, as he showed no self-consciousness about taking up another art form.

Painting also became an escape from the pressures of Broadway. Largely because the extravagant Ziegfeld style and the satirical book of "Show Girl," from a J. P. McEvoy novel, simply didn't meld, this musical was only a mild success, and the result was a full-blown row, even a threatened lawsuit by George and Ira, before they were paid. They never worked for Ziegfeld again. The unfinished "East is West" was never produced.

As always, George's work was little affected. Playwright Morrie Ryskind reworked the book done by George S. Kaufman for "Strike Up the Band," to soften it a little, George and Ira re-worked

Gershwin's interest in art began with his new Riverside Drive apartment, about 1928. At the suggestion of his cousin, Henry Botkin, a well-known painter, he began collecting art and soon became passionately addicted to sketching and painting himself. Beginning with still lifes and landscapes, he soon turned to portraiture, which proved to be his true metier. Left, with his first attempt at oil painting, a portrait of Emily Paley. Below, his technical advance can be seen in this 1932 self-portrait in evening clothes. Bottom left, from his collection, "Jazz Musicians," by Chapin.

30

In 1932 the Pulitzer Prize for drama was awarded for the first time to a musical, but only to the "book" writers, George S. Kaufman and Morrie Ryskind, and the lyricist, Ira Gershwin. There was then no Pulitzer award-ed for music. Below, letter from Columbia University's president informing Ira of his Pulitzer Prize. Bottom, star comedian Bobby Clark woos a lady (Kathryn Hamill) in the second version of "Strike Up The Band."

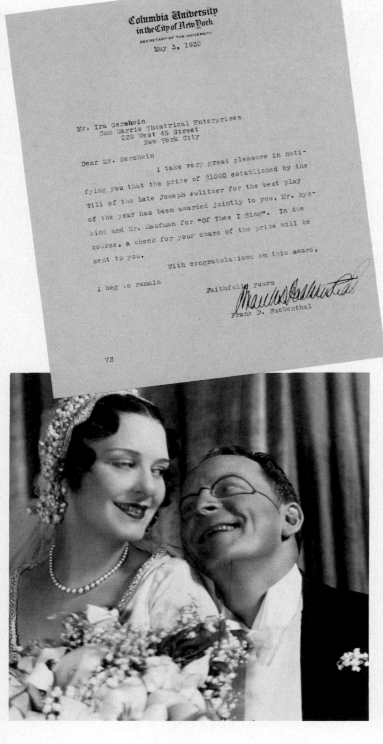

Columbia University
in the City of New York
SECRETARY OF THE UNIVERSITY
May 3, 1932

Mr. Ira Gershwin
Sam Harris Theatrical Enterprises
239 West 45 Street
New York City

Dear Mr. Gershwin

I take very great pleasure in notifying you that the prize of $1000 established by the will of the late Joseph Pulitzer for the best play of the year has been awarded jointly to you, Mr. Ryskind and Mr. Kaufman for "Of Thee I Sing". In due course, a check for your share of the prize will be sent to you.

With congratulations on this award,

I beg to remain

Faithfully yours
Frank D. Fackenthal

VS

the score, and in Depression 1930, what hadn't suited audiences in 1927 became a Broadway hit. Although not obvious then, it can be seen now that the Gershwin style really belonged not to the Gilded Jazz Age but to the bitter 1930's. The Depression swept away facile sentimentality, and the anti-war satire suited the new mood.

The same year, the Gershwins produced their mock-Western, "Girl Crazy." Instead of a super-sweet Marilyn Miller, the musical made a star out of pert Ginger Rogers. Onto the stage strode for the first time that queen of brass voices, Ethel Merman, to bring down the house with "I Got Rhythm." The orchestra was a brass band, led by Red Nichols and including such players as Benny Goodman, Gene Krupa, Glenn Miller, Jimmy Dorsey and Jack Teagarden!

Now a new field of endeavor beckoned. The movies had acquired sound, and the studios were all doing musicals. Fox wanted to add music to the appeal of its hit team of Janet Gaynor and Charles Farrell, and late in 1930 the newspapers were publicizing the departure of George and Ira Gershwin, with Ira's wife, Leonore, for Hollywood. The now-forgotten comedy, called "Delicious," had the Gaynor-Farrell charm, but for a dream sequence about New York, George wrote a six-minute orchestral background with a rivet theme. He decided to use it as the core of a major work for symphony orchestra.

Although he had led an active, enjoyable life in California, Gershwin was glad to return to New York. He brought with him the piano score for what was to become the "Second Rhapsody" and some work for a new Broadway musical. Much encouraged by the success of "Strike Up the Band," George S. Kaufman and Morrie Ryskind planned a political satire, and in December, 1931 came "Of Thee I Sing," the first musical to win a Pulitzer Prize and the first in which George and Ira completely integrated text and music.

"No verse and chorus songs," said Ira, who shared the prize with Kaufman and Ryskind. George received no prize, as there was then no Pulitzer for music. Not that he minded—both brothers always rejoiced in each other's successes. What delighted George was the 441-performance run, a success that saved the Music Box theater for his friends Irving Berlin and Sam H. Harris, who were about to lose it in the Depression.

He took breath from Broadway for a while. His income now freed him to begin a more extended

Both art and the creation of theater music filled George Gershwin's life, even while he continued to study and compose classically. Working in pastels gave him confidence to progress to oils. Left, two pastel portrait sketches Gershwin did in 1930, the top one simply labeled "Sydney," the lower one of Ira Gershwin, with the added humorous comment, "Lyric Writer?" Below, scenes from two successful shows, the political campaign scene from "Of Thee I Sing" (1931) and, at bottom, Ethel Merman in "Girl Crazy" (1930) with the Western saloon pianist, Roger Edens. Merman leaped to stardom in this show.

period of study, with Joseph Schillinger. In January, 1932, the "Second Rhapsody" had its premiere with the Boston Symphony Orchestra under Serge Koussevitsky, with Gershwin as soloist, to the usual divided critical response. George also saw to completion a project suggested by young publisher Richard Simon, "The George Gershwin Song Book." He conducted and played in a concert at the Metropolitan Opera House. On a vacation in Havana, he found inspiration for a new tone poem, "Rumba," later revised as "Cuban Overture."

At this moment of career triumph, however, life took a more serious turn. The first break in the family circle occurred, when on May 15 Morris Gershwin died. Giving up plans for another European trip, Gershwin submerged his grief in activity.

"Rumba" was premiered at a Lewisohn Stadium night that was the first all-Gershwin concert. Nearly 18,000 people attended, a Stadium record, to hear Gershwin play both of his rhapsodies and to applaud "Rumba." But the Depression was deepening everywhere, ominous events in Europe were clouding the horizon, and even Gershwin's sanguine nature seemed to grow restless.

From the late Twenties, George Gershwin's theater and concert activities increased. His producers on Broadway were Vinton Freedley, left below, and Alex Aarons. Noted conductors were glad to conduct concerts in which he appeared, such as Fritz Reiner, shown left in cen-ter photo with Gershwin, critic-composer Deems Taylor and famed arranger Robert Russell Bennett before a Lewisohn Stadium concert. Bottom, facade today of 33 Riverside Drive, where Gershwin moved in 1928 to an Art Deco-decorated penthouse apartment.

He abandoned the penthouse of which he had been so proud for a 14-room duplex on New York's upper-class East Side. As if closing the door on the Twenties, he discarded Art Deco furnishing for traditional English-gentry style. Persuaded by Alex Aarons and Vinton Freedley to do a show for them, in hopes of recouping their Depression-ravaged fortunes, which had ended with their losing the Alvin Theater which they had built, George and Ira reluctantly took on the job.

But "Pardon My English" had a bad book, and the Gershwins themselves had taught Broadway to expect better. The show failed. So did many others in the destruction of the theater world by the Depression. Despite the sturdy character of both George and Ira, in their different ways, the miasma of 1933, perhaps the worst year of the decade, seeped into their work. "Let 'Em Eat Cake," a sequel to "Of Thee I Sing," had a bitterness not found in the good-natured satire of the first show. The song, "Down With Everything That's Up" expressed the mood all too well for audiences seeking escape from reality when they went to a musical.

Gershwin continued to be restless, He was now 35, and in his Victorian sub-conscious an unmarried 35-year-old man was an irresponsible lightweight. The Twentieth Century part of him had skipped gaily through the Twenties, when everything in manners and morals was being turned upside down, but he remained a Victorian, although fond, brother toward his sister Frances. He had such Victorian ideas about marriage that he had entirely put off Rosamund Walling, much as she admired him.

Now, in his thirties, he was involved with Kay Swift, a very attractive musician and composer who often assisted him. He had known her for several years as the wife of James Warburg, but after her divorce, she became his closest woman friend. Both he and Kay talked about marriage with their mutual friend, Emil Mosbacher, a young financier, but somehow it never happened.

Gershwin was well aware of his own ambivalence about marriage and his concern led to his starting psychoanalysis in 1934. The idea was typically

ALVIN THEATRE

52ND STREET
West of Broadway

UNDER THE DIRECTION OF
ALEX. A. AARONS & VINTON FREEDLEY

In 1927, Aarons and Freedley built the Alvin Theater, which is shown below in a contemporary rendering. They had a special program cover designed, shown left as it looked for "Funny Face" that year. Even after they had lost their theater in the Depression, it housed "Porgy and Bess" in 1935.

Left, middle, Gershwin in the Beverly Hills house he rented on his first Hollywood trip in 1930. Bottom, two views of his Riverside Drive apartment. His painter cousin Henry Botkin did the bedroom screen in an impressionistic interpretation of "An American in Paris."

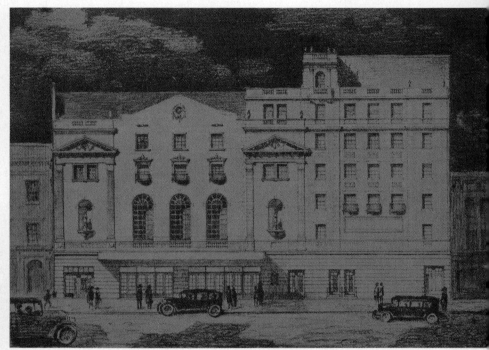

In 1925, Du Bose Heyward, a literarily talented Charleston, South Carolina aristocrat, wrote a novel, "Porgy," about the Gullah Negro life of the coast. Its vivid scenes captured George Gershwin's imagination as an opera subject, but in 1926 Heyward and his wife turned it into a play. They are shown *below at the time of the play's production. Not until 1934 did Gershwin write his opera, going to a Charleston coast island for the summer. He sketched his primitive sleep-and-work room on Folly Island, bottom, whose conditions he didn't mind at all.*

American, for in no other country had Freudianism taken so strong and rapid a hold. Of course, George's analyst had to be one of the most famous of the day, Dr. Gregory Zilboorg. As involved in the arts as he was in science, Zilboorg soon became a good friend.

Not that the psychoanalysis lasted all that long. At first, Gershwin took five sessions a week, but when it didn't seem to solve his problems after a year Gershwin grew impatient. Repeating his pattern of taking instruction from the best man but breaking off when he grew dissatisfied, Gershwin stopped analysis.

Perhaps his own instinct for action when a crisis loomed was soundest after all. With his beloved Broadway seemingly unable to supply the kind of subject he and Ira could take to, was it finally time to really get down to writing an opera?

He had read the novel "Porgy," by a South Carolina aristocrat, Du Bose Heyward, back in 1926. The story of simple life among Gullah Negroes, a group unknown to George, who knew only Harlem, excited both his sympathy with blacks and his interest in an exotic locale. He had written at once to Heyward that he wanted to turn "Porgy" into an opera, but would need years to prepare himself for such a task.

A gentle, poetically talented Charleston aristocrat who had suffered both polio and genteel poverty,

Heyward was intrigued, but informed Gershwin that a play of "Porgy" was being produced by the Theater Guild. He and his equally talented wife, Dorothy Kuhns Heyward, wrote the play, which became a great success. Meanwhile, in 1929, Gershwin had been signed by Otto Kahn to write an opera for the Metropolitan on "The Dybbuk," a European Jewish legend, but the project had aborted.

Now it was 1932, with the Depression all but killing the Metropolitan Opera, yet Gershwin wrote to Heyward that he would now like to start on "Porgy." After certain prior rights and complications were cleared, a contract was signed with the Theater Guild. Determined that "Porgy" would belong to its creators, both Gershwin brothers and Dubose Heyward put up money of their own. Their faith went unrewarded, as the 124 performances of "Porgy and Bess," as the work was re-titled to avoid confusion with the play, didn't make back its cost.

"Porgy and Bess" took two concentrated years of creation for all three collaborators. As usual, George and Ira enchanted a man very different from themselves, as Heyward recorded, and the unlikely trio had no trouble using their diverse talents. The reception of "Porgy and Bess" was something else. The critics didn't know what to make of it. Both music and drama critics reviewed it. The music critics said it wasn't serious enough for an opera and the drama critics said it was too serious for Broadway. Each seemed to be demanding what they were used to, and "Porgy and Bess" didn't fit any of their formulas.

THE LAST YEARS

Not a whit daunted, Gershwin showed an unusually combative attitude toward his critics, writing in defense of his work. Not a "serious" opera? He retorted that it was a "folk" opera and that he had created a new form. The solos were only song hits? He pointed out that conventional arias were also song hits.

About the hits there was no doubt. "Porgy and Bess" was gone by the spring following its opening on October 10, 1935, but by mid-1936 Lawrence Tibbett and Helen Jepson, leading Metropolitan Opera stars, had recorded the opera's big numbers. Soon concert sopranos everywhere were putting "Summertime" on their programs. Tibbett made "I've Got Plenty o' Nuthin'" a staple encore number for his recitals.

George never saw another performance of "Porgy and Bess," but he remained confident the work would live. More important for the moment was to find a new project. The answer came from Holly-

Kay Swift, musician and composer, who helped with the work of transcribing the score of "Porgy and Bess," is shown below in the 1920's at her and her husband's upstate New York farm, where George sought peace for earlier composing. She was then the wife of banker James *Warburg, but after her divorce in the 1930's became Gershwin's closest woman friend, as she could share his musical interests as others could not. His last apartment in New York was a duplex in this building, bottom, on East 72nd Street, seen as it looks today.*

wood, where old friends Fred Astaire and Ginger Rogers had become an important star team.

Their producer at RKO Studios, Pandro S. Berman, had already given them films with music by Cole Porter, Irving Berlin and Jerome Kern. The Gershwins had remained elusive until now. With the Broadway future still Depression-clouded, they decided to venture once more to Hollywood, even promising to write two films.

George was of two minds about Hollywood. He enjoyed the climate, as he could play golf and tennis constantly. He could indulge his painting interests with Edward G. Robinson, the star who was a notable art collector. He even found a new colony of music people, some refugees from Nazism.

One of these he had already aided, the much-respected leader of the modernist school, composer Arnold Schoenberg. In 1933 Gershwin had contributed to scholarships for students to study with Schoenberg at his first American refuge, the Malkin Conservatory in Boston. Now Schoenberg was heading the music department at the University of California in Los Angeles. It seemed that the austere-looking Schoenberg was as much of a tennis fan as George was, and they were soon regular players.

However, all this could not make up for the descent from the high mountain of creating "Porgy and Bess" to the rigidities of studio life. As he well knew from his earlier Hollywood experience, he and Ira might create masterpieces only to see the studio do what it liked with them.

Even with the pleasure of working with Fred and Ginger, it wasn't enough. He went back to New York for two all-Gershwin nights at the Lewisohn Stadium during the summer of 1936, and did several West Coast concerts. Friends noticed moods of depression, something quite new for him.

Nothing, however, affected his work. His score for "Shall We Dance?" was as brilliant as any of his Broadway shows, as was the music for "A Damsel in Distress," in which Astaire had a new co-star, Joan Fontaine.

Although longing to return to New York, and evidently determined to continue with concert and opera composing, Gershwin agreed to write a film for Samuel Goldwyn. However, more than spells of depression were beginning to bother him.

In February, 1937, while playing the "Concerto in F" with Alexander Smallens directing the Los Angeles Philharmonic, Gershwin suffered a momentary memory lapse, during which he seemed to smell burning rubber. He telephoned Dr. Zilboorg, who correctly diagnosed some physical cause, but a check-up showed nothing.

Re-union in Hollywood with Fred Astaire and Ginger Rogers came in 1936. They are shown, opposite page, with dance director Hermes Pan, left, director Mark Sandrich and Ira Gershwin, in back of George, on the set of "Shall We Dance?" Below, George Gershwin conducts a rehearsal of the Los Angeles Symphony Orchestra for one of his last concerts, early in 1937. The great conductor, Pierre Monteux, was his collaborator in the series, which soothed his restlessness at having no classical project on hand. In California, George re- newed his earlier ac- quaintance with re- nowned composer Arnold Schoenberg. They now became daily tennis part- ners and constant music conversationalists. Gershwin began painting Schoenberg, and is seen below completing the por- trait, the last work he fin- ished. Left, the portrait itself, now in the Library of Congress Music Divi- sion as part of their Gershwin collection. It was donated by Ira Gershwin in his later years when he established the collection with origi- nal scores, manuscripts and photographs.

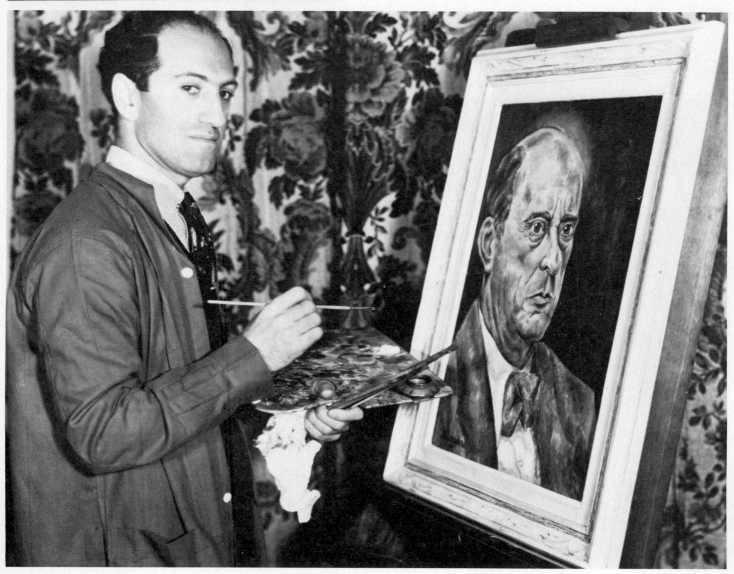

The last known photo of George Gershwin, below, shows him playing at a recital for RKO Studio executives in June, 1937. Bottom, working on the Goldwyn Follies, with producer Sam Goldwyn, right, listening through earphones to the recorded sound of the orchestra conducted by Alfred Newman.

Right, arranger-composer Ferde Grofé and his wife arrive at George's funeral service, Temple Emanu-El, New York. Although older than Gershwin, Grofé began composing on George's encouragement, had orchestrated "Rhapsody in Blue" back in 1924, and regarded him with affectionate gratitude.

George finished "A Damsel in Distress" without trouble, and in May started on "The Goldwyn Follies." He was not to finish it. Only a month later he began suffering from headaches and dizzy spells. Still, X-ray techniques of that day revealed nothing, although the doctors were now urging a spinal tap to detect a possible tumor.

The end came dreadfully fast. On July 11, 1937, after an operation which could not remove all of a fast-growing malignant brain tumor, George Gershwin, not yet 39, died.

THE WORLD MOURNS

The reaction to his death reveals either a better time, when a composer's death could stop the world's heart beating for a moment or the tremendous impact he had made on an era searching for interpreters. Thousands of newspapers all over the world headlined his passing. He had two funeral services—one in Hollywood, the other in New York. They were timed to start together so that at that moment all work in every Hollywood studio stopped for a minute of silence.

It rained in New York, as if the city mourned. Not only did 3,500 people jam Temple Emanu-El, but over a thousand more gathered outside. Mayor Fiorello LaGuardia headed the list of honorary pallbearers, joined by that symbol of the Twenties, former mayor James J. Walker, Walter Damrosch, George M. Cohan, Edwin Franko Goldman, Vernon Duke, Al Jolson and Sam H. Harris. (Duke was to finish "The Goldwyn Follies.")

Recently, Rabbi Nathan A. Perilman, who officiated at the funeral, wrote this author:

"I remember vividly the funeral service of George Gershwin. The main sanctuary was filled to overflowing, and, of course, there was the enormous sadness. Here was a young man who was cut down in the prime of his life. It was an enormous tragedy, and one could feel this sense of anguish throughout the temple. Rabbi Stephen Samuel Wise delivered

Rabbi Nathan A. Perilman, left, officiated at the funeral. Among honorary pallbearers was then-Mayor Fiorello H. LaGuardia, left in top photo below. Further down the line, in wing collar, is Irving Caesar, George's early lyricist. Bottom, among the mourners awaiting the removal of the casket, at right,

Vernon Duke, next to policeman. Duke had been a close friend ever since arriving from Russia as Vladimir Dukelsky in the early Twenties. Not only did Gershwin sponsor Duke in becoming a popular song composer, but gave him his Anglicized name. Duke finished "The Goldwyn Follies."

Al Jolson, near right, and former Mayor James J. Walker, seen arriving at Temple Emanu-El. Below, Ethel Merman greets then-Governor Herbert H. Lehman, and conductor Alexander Smallens welcomes Mrs. Lehman to Lewisohn Stadium for the memori-al concert of August 8, 1937. At bottom, pall-bearers solemnly remove the flower-laden casket from Temple Emanu-El. At right, fourth in, hat over heart, Al Jolson is seen, while at left, in wing collar, Irving Caesar waits.

A family mausoleum, bottom, was built by Mrs. Rose Gershwin around 1940 in a Westchester cemetery. Today, she, the three Gershwin sons, and their father are all interred within. Top, interior of the mausoleum, showing George's site, left wall, and on sill of stained-glass window, bronze urn holding the ashes of Leopold Godowsky, husband of sister Frances. The cemetery is one where a number of theater celebrities, such as producer Billy Rose, are buried. It is notable that the mausoleum, although a family structure, carries George Gershwin's name over the entrance.

the eulogy, as only he could have. It was a magnificent tribute.

"In retrospect, we can say that George Gershwin was a rare blend of several souls—there was something in him of the European classicist, the American black and the Eastern European Jew. Musically, he combined those three elements into a unique harmony and synthesis, never really duplicated."

Todd Duncan, star of "Porgy and Bess," remembered that after the service "I saw a man walking with his head down in the middle of Fifth Avenue . . . on the white line directly between the lanes of traffic . . . it was Al Jolson and I watched him keep on walking, oblivious to all around him."

Other composers, many of whom had been encouraged by Gershwin, felt what Ferde Grofé called "an irreparable loss."

Arnold Schoenberg confounded his own admirers by writing a sincere appreciation of Gershwin: "Many musicians do not consider George Gershwin a serious composer. But they should understand that, serious or not, he is a composer—that is, a man who lives in music and expresses everything, serious or not, sound or superficial, by means of music, because it is his native language."

The man himself was as deeply mourned as the composer. George S. Kaufman, that normally cynical wit, wrote a mutual friend, "George's death was a tragedy, the greatest I have ever known." Many years later, his early lyricist, Irving Caesar, said, "He was in a class by himself! Isn't that enough?"

On August 8, 1937, 20,000 people gathered at Lewisohn Stadium for one of the many memorial concerts that were soon held. George's secretary, Nanette Kutner, looking around the vast crowd, thought, "George, you made your one mistake! It was to die."

Edward G. Robinson gave the eulogy at the same concert: "I value above all things the memory I have of George Gershwin."

So shocked was George Gershwin's whole generation that novelist John O'Hara could well have been speaking for them all with his reaction to the news of that tragic death: "I don't have to believe it if I don't want to!"

George and sister Frances in the late 1920's exchanged portraits with loving inscriptions, George adding a bar of music to his. Below, George himself took this picture, the only known one of the parents and all three sons—left to right, George, Rose, Arthur, Morris and Ira. This page, George composing at his 72nd Street apartment, is seen with the portrait he did in 1933 of the little daughter of Paul, his valet, shown below in George's pastel sketch. The child's painting, shown at left, is today in the apartment of Arthur Gershwin's widow in New York.

THE CLASSICAL GERSHWIN

Undoubtedly the most remarkable fact about George Gershwin's concert and opera music is the impact created in relation to its small quantity. His entire output can be briefly listed: Rhapsody in Blue, Concerto in F, Preludes for Piano, An American in Paris, Second Rhapsody, Cuban Overture, Variations on 'I Got Rhythm,' and Porgy and Bess.

Yet each of these creations was an occasion at the time of its premiere, was much debated, even fought over, and has continued to be performed with increasing frequency, in other countries as well as his own. Few other composers with so small an output have made so singular an impression.

His first public effort, in 1922, was the one-act opera, "Blue Monday," oddly placed in one of George White's "Scandals."

It was significant chiefly for its being based on black life, although of Harlem, not the Southern scene he would use later. After all, he had known Harlem since childhood and evidently always felt at ease with blacks.

Like many another stage work, "Blue Monday" was unceremoniously yanked from the show after its single performance. But Paul Whiteman never forgot it, and in 1925 he gave it in a concert performance, and again in 1936, when Ferde Grofé made a new orchestration. What was it which impressed these well-trained musicians?

Gershwin hadn't produced an integrated work on the order of a "Cavalleria Rusticana," even if his libretto was based on the same kind of erotic jealousies. The score is rather a series of songs linked by jazz-influenced recitative. Of the songs, "Blue Monday Blues," "Has Anyone Seen Joe," and the spiritual-inspired "I'm Going to See My Mother" all show what Gershwin was searching for. But it was that search, in its move toward using blues and jazz for serious effect, which impressed Grofé and Whiteman.

Whiteman had begun his musical career as first violinist with symphony orchestras, so he understood the fierce musical battles of the time over modern music. The combatants often didn't know too clearly what they meant by such terms as "dissonance," or "jazz." Whiteman himself was publicized as "The King of Jazz," and seemingly believed that his music was jazz.

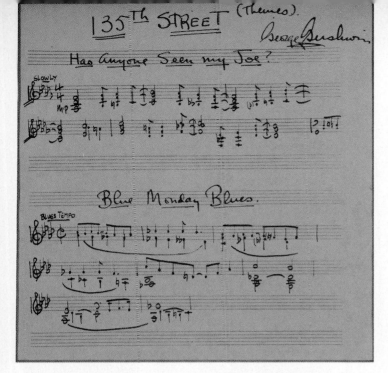

135TH STREET (Themes).
George Gershwin

Has Anyone Seen my Joe?

Blue Monday Blues.

Left, opening lines of two "arias" from "Blue Monday," as presented by Gershwin to dear friends Mabel and Bob Schirmer. Twelve years later, primitive Folly Island, South Carolina, below, sketched by Henry Botkin, who accompanied him in 1934 for a summer of composing "Porgy and Bess." George's concert life included his own famous performances. Left, he appeared in a Steinway piano advertisement. Bottom, in 1929, with conductor Fritz Reiner, center, and Metropolitan Opera star tenor Richard Crooks, for a solo appearance with the Cincinnati Symphony.

Like his music, George Gershwin's pianism appealed to audiences for both popular and classical music. In 1930 showman S. L. Rothafel signed Gershwin to play onstage at his Roxy Theater, New York, along with Paul Whiteman's film, "King of Jazz." Below, top, left to right, arranger Ferde

Grofé, Gershwin, Rothafel, Whiteman, rehearsing. As a classical pianist, he began in 1927 appearing at Lewisohn Stadium, New York, a huge classical amphitheater built for outdoor summer concerts in a non-air conditioned world. Bottom, at a rehearsal piano in the stadium.

MUSIC CONFLICTS RAGE

In truth, the term "jazz" was used very loosely. Any strongly rhythmic music, including much use of syncopation, and played on saxophones or other brass instruments, was called "jazz." As it had risen from dance halls, strictly repeated rhythm was often the rule, making much popular music sound simplistic to classically trained musicians. Unlike ragtime, which had preceded jazz, and was a sort of cousin, jazz included a good deal of "dissonance," and "dissonance" had been a fighting word since 1900 in musical circles. It signified the new school of European classical composers which the American musical establishment violently opposed. The same men who hurled thunderbolts of critical displeasure against jazz fought against the twelve-tone scale and serial music of Arnold Schoenberg and Igor Stravinsky.

To the Yankee musical establishment, the melting pot of New York was not "American." How could immigrant Jews such as George Gershwin, Aaron Copland or Ernest Bloch, all not even college-trained, create an "American" music? Of course, the New Yorkers fought back. Such younger critics as Gilbert Seldes, Carl Van Vechten, Deems Taylor and John Hammond not only championed jazz but insisted on the entry of so-called jazz elements in composing "serious" music. When the Yankee musical establishment decried what it thought were the twin influences of the Negro and the Jew, New York commentators insisted on the American value of both and whatever other influences might come out of the melting pot.

Into this boiling fury of dispute George Gershwin stepped almost blithely in 1924 with "Rhapsody in Blue." Its very opening sounded like a challenge—a clarinet glissando rising to the sky above. The form of the whole piece was deliberately loose. One critic referred to its "whoop of an introduction" and concluded·that "there is an element of inevitability about his piece."

The phrase is a happy one. "Rhapsody in Blue" was one of those compositions that once written seems to have been necessary to music. Gershwin took the work seriously, despite the speed with which he had to write it. At the first complete rehearsal some thirty guests were invited, mostly

music critics, but also conductor Walter Damrosch and Victor Herbert, the monarch of melodious European-style operetta. He was deeply impressed, and suggested how the middle melody might be made more effective by giving it a preceding rising passage. As they were always to be with Gershwin, the critics were divided, with the older men lukewarm, the younger ones more enthusiastic.

In the original score, the opening passage appears as separate notes, since a glissando on the clarinet is difficult to play. One day, as a humorous protest at any further rehearsing, Whiteman's clarinetist, Ross Gorman, played the passage as a glissando wail. Gershwin at once adopted it. He was always to be open to advice and suggestions from performers and musicians whom he respected.

It has been said that the form of the "Rhapsody in Blue" came from Liszt, the major melody harks back to Tchaikovsky, and in the harmonic elements can be heard Debussy and Chopin. But if so, the various influences are melded and transformed into something wholly American. It is a mixture of the brashness of the 1920's in New York and the romanticism of the late nineteenth century in which Gershwin was born, and somehow it works.

In the 1920's it seemed the very voice of that restless, longing decade, but today it is simply the voice of George Gershwin. He was then hailed as the composer who would, indeed, bring jazz and classicism together, but he, himself, knew better. That melodic gift, Tchaikovskian or not, was never to desert him.

On August 26, 1929, Gershwin made his debut as a conductor; bottom, rehearsing at Lewisohn Stadium, with Willem Hoogstraaten, right, the orchestra's regular conductor. Above, the 1927 party given so Maurice Ravel (at piano) could meet George Gershwin: left to right, conductor Oscar Fried, Eva Gauthier, the hostess, Tedesco of the San Carlo Opera, Naples, and Gershwin.

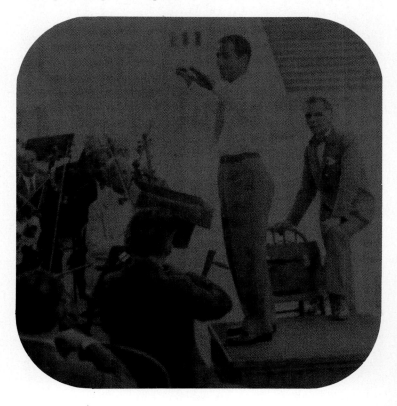

Gershwin's life was always filled with family and friends even while working. Below, snapped in upstate New York with Mabel Schirmer, who with her husband was among the constant visitors to George and Ira's composing "retreat." Bottom, family party in Belmar, New Jersey, June, 1926, for Emily and Lou Paley's sixth wedding anniversary. George posed everybody and then stretched out in front. Directly above George's head is Emily Paley, and to her right, Phil Charig, rehearsal pianist for George's shows, Leonore and Ira Gershwin. Top row, second from left, Lou Paley. Emily was Leonore's sister.

"Rhapsody in Blue" literally flew around the world. A million copies of a shortened version on records were sold. Several hundred thousand copies of the published score sold, plus uncounted numbers of various transcriptions. Both Paul Whiteman and George Gershwin were staggered by the enormous success of what they had both seen as a small experiment that might convince the classical music world in New York that jazz was a legitimate part of modern music.

Walter Damrosch, conductor of the New York Symphony Society, was one of those looking for new American voices in modern music. Impressed by the "Rhapsody," he persuaded the society to commission a work from Gershwin, and in July, 1925, despite doing three Broadway musicals that year, George began work on what he at first called "New York Concerto." He had given "Rhapsody in Blue" a first title of "American Rhapsody," seeming in both instances to be making a statement on the side of his school of modernist music.

But Gershwin was never personally contentious, and when his brother Ira suggested less challenging titles, he changed them. He did let get around a story that when he decided to write a concerto he went out and bought a book to find out what a concerto was. It was the kind of mischief he liked to make, as if to twit the musical establishment with their stuffy insistence on academic training. What he really did was to study a number of the standard classic concertos in his typically pragmatic manner, always preferring to go straight to practice rather than theory.

That summer of 1925 Gershwin went to the old American cultural center of Chautauqua, New York, at the invitation of Ernest Hutcheson, who conducted master classes in piano there. Gershwin needed some time away from the demands of his theater career, because he was going to orchestrate the concerto himself. The only adverse criticism of the "Rhapsody in Blue" which he had taken to heart had been the sneers that a Broadway composer couldn't really write serious music when he needed another man to do half the work. Although always ready to accept expert help and suggestions, Gershwin never again allowed any other hand to orchestrate his concert compositions.

He accomplished the bulk of the Concerto, but the completion date on the manuscript is November 10. Evidently, he had been impressed by Paul Whiteman's preview rehearsals of "Rhapsody in Blue," as he now hired, on his own, an orchestra of 60 musicians for a runthrough, with his friend Bill Daly to conduct and Walter Damrosch as his audience. Both Daly and Damrosch suggested some revisions and excisions, largely with the aim of tightening up the composition. George's love of improvisation always threatened to run away with him. But the changes were comparatively minor and on December 3 the New York Symphony, conducted by Walter Damrosch and with George Gershwin as soloist, gave "Concerto in F" its premiere.

Gershwin himself described the concerto as being in "sonata form-but. . ." There are three movements, each characterized by its tempo, in the classic manner, but both structure and content are free and unconventional. The first movement (Allegro) opens not with an orchestral statement and development of basic themes but with snatches of jazz atmospherics and dancelike motifs in woodwinds and kettledrums. They serve to lead into three successive themes, a lively bassoon figure with full orchestra, a blues-influenced theme for piano, and a typically Gershwin melody in broad, flowing waltz time for strings and the piano weaving around it.

The second movement (Andante) is dominated by song-like themes, contrasting sharply with the final movement (Allegro con brio), which erupts into rhythmic and colorful themes. Gershwin uses the full symphony orchestra plus a bass drum, snare drum, cymbals, "Charleston stick," bells and xylophone, but notably no saxophones. As he said, he was the last romantic, not a "jazz" composer, even if he used jazz elements.

Despite divided critical reaction, audience enthusiasm for "Concerto in F" ran high, and it was soon accepted in Europe. Five years later the eminent English conductor, Albert Coates, made a list of what he thought were the fifty best musical works of modern times. Only one American work was included, the Gershwin "Concerto in F." A classical standard by now, it has also appealed as ballet music, most notably in the setting by Jerome Robbins for the New York City Ballet.

Having proved that "Rhapsody in Blue" wasn't just a single lucky stroke, Gershwin was now surrounded by admirers giving him much well-

The Riverside Drive apartment was carefully divided into work and entertaining areas. Work centered on his Steinway grand, seen above about 1930, with two of his new art collection pieces. Bottom, Gershwin in a Vienna portrait, 1928, typically avoiding the camera and almost unsmiling.

An early member of the American Society of Authors and Composers (ASCAP) which protects composers' rights, Gershwin is seen above in Washington, 1936, in testimony on copyright issues, with, left to right, Rudy Vallee, Irving Berlin and Gene Buck, then ASCAP president. Critic, jazz enthusiast and able amateur photographer Carl Van Vechten took the portrait of Gershwin, below, in 1932.

intentioned but contradictory advice. However, he continued on his own way, taking new counterpoint lessons from Henry Cowell, one of the much-debated modernist composers, and continuing his busy theater career. He never agreed that there was a gulf between the two kinds of music—if both theater and concert music composing came easily to him, why not do both?

In fact, in the next three years after "Concerto in F" he was so busy theatrically that he produced only "Five Preludes For Piano" as concert composing. Oddly enough, they remain the only work he ever produced for piano alone. He had actually completed several short piano pieces back in 1924, calling them "Novelettes." Two of them were subsequently transcribed for violin and piano for the violinist Samuel Dushkin in a single composition called "Short Story." Not until a 1926 concert did Gershwin polish all five and play them as originally intended, for piano alone.

Three of the preludes were published, and remain frequently performed. The first (Allegretto ben ritmato e deciso) combines dance elements in a characteristically bold rhythmic manner. The second uses a C-sharp minor blues-influenced melody in the noble style Gershwin could always summon for concert work. Rhythm again accents the third prelude, but in a manner more joyous than the first prelude. The remaining two preludes are still in manuscript, but have been recorded by Michael Tilson Thomas.

A WORLD FIGURE

When Gershwin made the famous European trip in 1928, he met in each city the leading composers of the day, many of whom gave him warmly inscribed photographs of themselves as mementos. Quite capable of understanding the avant-garde work of composers very different from himself, Gershwin at once became friendly with Alban Berg in Vienna, a man-of-the-world equally able to admire Gershwin's work. Below, the portrait which Berg inscribed to Gershwin, including music from his own "Lyric Suite," a piece Gershwin particularly liked. He also first met Arnold Schoenberg on this trip.

As George Gershwin's theater work brought him as much attention as did his concert compositions (after "Concerto in F" he had composed both "Oh, Kay!" and "Funny Face") he could fairly be called the most famous musical figure in the world of the later 1920s. Although always amiable about being interviewed and photographed, he wanted a vacation, especially as he was conceiving his first work entirely for symphony orchestra.

With this idea in mind, Gershwin went to Europe early in 1928 with his brother Ira and Ira's wife, Leonore. The trip hardly turned out to be private, from the first day of shipboard photographs by the New York papers through constant socializing and attending musical events in London, Paris and Vienna. He was as lionized in Europe as in New York, and as his sociable nature enjoyed friends and parties, the European visit was a great success.

George particularly loved Paris, as Paris loved him. They were playing "Rhapsody in Blue" even in weird arrangements. More interesting was a ballet to the piece by the great choreographer-dancer Anton Dolin, who danced the lead in a conception depicting the struggle between jazz and classical music. Dolin, as Jazz, triumphed, of course.

The European premiere of "Concerto in F" took place at the Paris Opera, with Gershwin present to hear Vladimir Golschmann conduct and Dimitri Tiomkin play the piano part. The concerto received an ovation and ecstatic reviews. Reading the French critics now, it seems that at least part of their enthusiasm arose from their eager desire to embrace what they saw as jazz. They were looking for jazz in serious music and that was enough.

As usual, what would seem to most people as a frantically busy schedule didn't in the least put Gershwin off from working on his new composition, which had now become an homage to Paris. Much taken with the varied sounds of Paris taxi horns, he decided to use real ones in the piece, and went all over the city with his friend Emily Schirmer to find some for purchase. They were on his hotel room piano one morning when two young music students, Mario Braggiotti and Jacques Fray, later to become a celebrated duo-piano team, called at his suite hoping just to meet him.

George was always cordial to any and all callers

52

As usual, George Gershwin didn't travel alone. On his European trip he went with Ira and Leonore Gershwin. Below, they are seen aboard ship on departure, as news photographers then regularly covered celebrity arrivals and departures on ocean liners. In Vienna, George also met the operetta composers, particularly

Franz Lehar, shown with him at bottom. Lehar's "The Merry Widow" had been a world success in George's boyhood, and they were photographed by a Viennese music magazine aware of the contrast between the two composers. Gershwin, however, could also admire the Lehar school of operetta.

and he invited the "boys" in. In a few minutes they noticed the taxi horns wonderingly, and Gershwin promptly handed them each one in different keys and sat down to play the opening theme of "An American in Paris," nodding for them to come in when wanted. Later, he was to help launch their career, but it was that morning which Braggiotti never forgot, playing those taxi horns for "such an illustrious composer."

Walter Damrosch had spoken for the new composition well before it had even begun to jell. Musicians always appreciated Gershwin more than did many critics. While in Vienna he met a number of older and younger composers, among them Alban Berg, whose highly modernist works George much admired. After playing for him, George was greatly surprised when Berg expressed enthusiasm for the Gershwin music.

"How can you possibly like my music when you write the kind of music you do?" Gershwin asked, to which Berg replied, "Music is music," showing a great deal more open-mindedness than many of the critics of the day. So did completely different composers, those of the Viennese operetta school, such as Emmerich Kalman and the great Franz Lehar, who welcomed Gershwin warmly.

AN AMERICAN IN PARIS

"An American in Paris" came under the classification of tone poem, meaning that it has a programmatic background and whatever form the composer chooses. Critic-composer Deems Taylor, in fact, wrote a very detailed scheme for the piece in the program for the concert of December 13, 1928 on which it was premiered, more detailed, in fact, than Gershwin had wanted. He preferred an impressionistic approach. "An American in Paris" is built on a series of themes, some fragmentary, others fully developed with symphonic elaboration. Jazz, blues and dance elements swirl in and out of it.

The premiere of "An American in Paris" met with the usual response to Gershwin's concert works—audience enthusiasm, bouquets and brickbats from the critics. Commentators from the Yankee establishment were infuriated by such "noises" as the taxi horns, part of a general trend among modernist composers to include the mechanistic sounds of modern life in their compositions, although many classical composers had used such realistic touches, even though of a gentler kind.

As with Gershwin's other works, the tone poem almost immediately became the favorite it has remained to this day. It has been several times adapted as a ballet, most notably by Gene Kelly in the film named for the work. In the New York artistic

world of 1928 it confirmed Gershwin's status as a leader in modern composing. At a celebratory party after the premiere, Otto H. Kahn, millionaire patron of the Metropolitan Opera, made a little speech as he presented George with a sterling silver humidor inscribed with the signatures of his many friends. Mr. Kahn not only praised Gershwin but practically begged him to deepen his art with the "tragedy" required for greatness.

Soon Kahn was offering to sponsor an opera by Gershwin for the Metropolitan Opera. George had been thinking along these lines, looking for a libretto. At first he had thought of doing one of the plays, common in the New York theater of his youth, about the immigrants in New York. With the Kahn offer, he turned to an old-world idea, a famous Yiddish play by S. Ansky, "The Dybbuk," about Polish Chassidic mysticism and supernaturalism. He had even begun notebook theme jottings when he learned that the rights to the play had already been taken by an Italian composer.

Busy with a new venture, conducting, he put aside the opera and went off to Hollywood to compose, with his brother Ira, a score for an early sound film at Fox. From the film, Gershwin used a six-minute segment as the essence of another major orchestral work. In Hollywood, he completed the piano score for what he called "New York Rhapsody." Back in New York, he orchestrated and revised it as "Rhapsody of Rivets." Following his now-established practice, he conducted it with a hired orchestra of 56 men in a studio lent him by the Na-

tional Broadcasting Company. The revisions after this rehearsal were few, but the title now became simply, "Second Rhapsody."

Undoubtedly, he was mindful of all the fuss about putting city sounds into music, and since the rivet idea was simply the first rhythmic subject for the piano, he was stating, by that simple title, that he had nothing further to prove about "jazz" in serious composing. Nevertheless, the "Second Rhapsody" is characteristically Gershwin in its blend of astringent rhythmic themes, dance-inspired melody (this time the rhumba) and the kind of stately, flowing melody saved from the sentimentalism of strings by the free use of brasses.

There was the touch of the unusual in his addition to the symphony orchestra of harp, xylophone, wood block and even a fly swatter! Gershwin always felt free to use whatever would get the precise effect he wanted. That didn't bother conductor Serge Koussevitsky a bit, as he was another champion of the modernist composers. He secured the "Second Rhapsody" for his Boston Symphony Orchestra, and with George as soloist, premiered it in January, 1932.

The Boston music critics greeted the "Second Rhapsody" with less than rapture, but the New York critics this time were generally enthusiastic. After all, eight years had passed since the "Rhapsody in Blue," during which their ears had been assaulted by far more "modernist" works than those of Gershwin's style. They still wanted to think that Gershwin was a "jazz" composer, but they were now willing to accept what they thought were jazz influences on serious composing.

Scarcely had Gershwin savored the new triumph than the first real tragedy of his life struck him. He had gone to Cuba for a brief vacation, bringing back some notes and actual instruments for a possible composition, and was planning another European trip when his father died on May 15. He turned to his work, first taking up the Cuban notes and completing in three weeks the piano score for what he at first called "Rumba," but which he soon retitled "Cuban Overture."

In three sections, with themes based on both rhumba and habanera dance influences, the overture is woven of both counterpoint and canon work. Its finale is a dynamic rhumba, using the Cuban instruments Gershwin had found there. His score specified that they should be placed in front of the orchestra: the Cuban stick, the Cuban hand drum, the gourd and the maracas. The premiere was to be at an outdoor concert in Lewisohn Stadium, and Gershwin knew well how sound could get lost there.

This concert was the first of the all-Gershwin programs which were to remain popular to the present day. Oscar Levant played the "Concerto in F," with William Daly conducting. Gershwin was the soloist in both of his rhapsodies, conducted by Albert Coates, who also conducted the Cuban-inspired orchestral composition.

The all-Gershwin concerts have remained unique in that he is still the only American composer to consistently be used for such events. Despite the fact that this means using the same compositions over and over, audiences never seem to tire of them. Perhaps because of his connection with the outdoor summer concerts at Lewisohn Stadium, they are still likely to be scheduled by summer symphony series, especially around July 4. Gershwin remains the most American of composers, except possibly for some of Aaron Copland's works.

The retitling of the "Rumba" occurred after Gershwin began to think that people would believe the work was some light piece of popular dance music. As the overture represented further advances in his handling of complex orchestral elements, he was evidently more and more conscious of broadening his knowledge and use of formal musical elements. The very next year he wrote "Variations on I Got Rhythm," which by using a theme already known emphasized sheer development.

Oscar Levant, below, first admired Gershwin music as a boy, attending "Ladies First" on tour in 1918. He became a New York jazz pianist, played "Rhapsody in Blue" for a 1925 recording, and subsequently was a valued friend. He played the "Concerto in F" at the first all-Gershwin concert in 1932 and remained a leading Gershwin interpreter throughout his career. Bottom, Gershwin with conductor Serge Koussevitsky at the time Koussevitsky secured the "Second Rhapsody" for the Boston Symphony Orchestra in early 1932. Koussevitsky was another champion of the modernist school of composers.

RADIO PERSONALITY

Radio had become a viable medium by the early Thirties, and it was a natural for Gershwin, even if his sponsor had to be a laxative company! He received $2,000 a program for the weekly "Music by Gershwin," for which this photograph, below left, was taken in early 1934. He needed money enough to work on his opera, particularly after losing his investment in a tour. Below, he is shown in Pittsburgh with the Leo Reisman orchestra on the twenty-eight city tour, a success whose money loss resulted from poor planning.

He wrote the work expressly for a tour that began in January, 1934, of twenty-eight cities with the Leo Reisman Orchestra, then a well-known ensemble. As Reisman fell ill, another leading conductor, Charles Previn, substituted, with Gershwin himself conducting "An American in Paris" and playing his "Concerto in F", "Rhapsody in Blue" and the new work.

Scored for full symphony orchestra, E-flat and B-flat saxophones, banjo and even Chinese gong, "Variations on I Got Rhythm" is a sheer display of technical virtuosity, a codification of the brilliant improvising Gershwin had so long been expert in performing with the piano alone. In the piece he changes the basic structure of the well-known theme, gives it moods varying from dynamic drive to mournful to joyous. The festive variation explodes in a dazzling display of orchestral work over and around the piano work.

The twenty-eight city tour was accomplished in less than a month. Within ten days, Gershwin launched a radio program, "Music by Gershwin," in which he was the whole show. However, with his customary generosity, he included other composers' work, some of them as yet relatively unknown. One was his own younger brother Arthur, who despite a prosperous career as a stockbroker, was devoted to music, but was too shy of George's renown to pursue a public career in that field until several years after his brother's death.

The program was undertaken by Gershwin quite simply to make money enough to live on while doing nothing except his opera. There had been losses, on shows that failed and even on the orchestral tour. George had been persuaded to be a partner in that venture, and ended up having to make up a loss of $5,000 because the manager had booked it into too many small auditoriums. The $2,000 a week he received for his radio efforts would subsidize his lifestyle for a year or two.

George Gershwin's opera began as a novel, "Porgy," by Du Bose Heyward, who with his wife Dorothy soon turned it into a successful play. Below, top, left to right, Percy Verwayne as Sportin' Life, Frank Wilson as Porgy and Evelyn Ellis as Bess in the 1926 Theater Guild production. Not until 1934 did Gershwin serious-ly work on the opera. Bottom, Heyward, left, and Ira Gershwin proved ideal collaborators on the libretto, each writing some parts alone, and at others writing together. The Charleston aristocrat was fascinated by the Gershwins and their easy, professional way of working.

As Gershwin had yet to write any concert music in the so-called larger forms, except the one concerto, his tackling of the giant task of an opera might well seem curious. But he had always been a theater man, and if Broadway had not been half-crippled by the Depression, he might well have built on the advances he had made in "Of Thee I Sing." He loved song, and the color of the stage.

Even before his aborted attempt with "The Dybbuk," he had been deeply interested in another subject. In 1926 he read a much-talked-about novel, "Porgy," by Du Bose Heyward, which so stirred him that he at once wrote to Heyward that he would like some day, when he was better prepared technically, to make an opera of it. In 1927, the Theater Guild successfully produced a play from the novel, so there was a script already in existence.

In 1932, when Gershwin had indeed become far more technically proficient in serious composition, he wrote Heyward again that after all the other ideas he had considered he still came back to "Porgy." Heyward, although not at all of Gershwin's world, was always interested, but when George still didn't make a definite start, he began considering other offers. The Charleston author was thinking along the lines of a musical rather than an opera, but the proposed musical, for Al Jolson, didn't attract him very much, if Gershwin would only write a "folk opera."

Although Jolson could have had Jerome Kern and Oscar Hammerstein II, the creators of "Show Boat," for his project, he and they withdrew when they learned of Gershwin's interest in the project, such was his reputation.

Even while still on his concert tour, Gershwin began a lively correspondence with Heyward and his wife, Dorothy, who was the author's collaborator on the play. George had previously visited Charleston twice to persuade both that "Porgy" had enough weight to stand up as an opera, and while he toured, Heyward began working on a libretto. Distance between them was an initial obstacle, as Heyward wouldn't leave Charleston and George was tied to New York by work on his new radio program.

The solution, as Heyward said himself, was Ira, who was always at George's side. It was a remark-

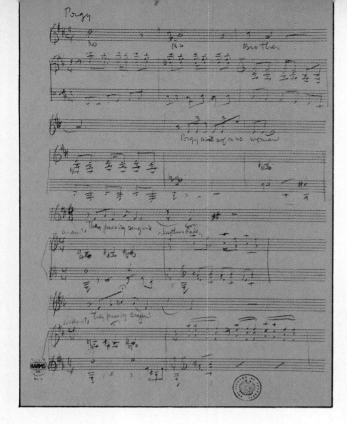

The complete original score of "Porgy and Bess" is now in the Library of Congress' Gershwin collection. Left, the opening of Porgy's entrance aria, "They Pass By Singing," in which he denies interest in Bess or any woman. George still managed, even while working intensely, as seen at bot-tom, to keep up his art interest. He sketched his room at Folly Island, paint-ed Ruby Elzy, a cast mem-ber of "Porgy," and on a brief vacation in Mexico after the opening, did the pastel sketch, below, of painter Diego Rivera, whose vivid work he greatly admired.

able collaboration, this trio of such different backgrounds and personalities. However, both George and Ira were easy to work with, completely professional men of the theater, and Heyward's gentle personality fitted in as if he had always known them.

All three approached the concept of a story about black life with a total lack of the racialism so prevalent at the time. As their letters show, they aimed simply at getting it right. Heyward's original novel had made a sensation because it was so straightforward one couldn't tell whether a black or a white had written it. George and Ira from boyhood had known New York black life as simply part of the metropolitan mosaic.

In the end, the libretto was by DuBose Heyward, with many suggestions from the Gershwins, largely on musical grounds, and the arias were by either Ira or Heyward, sometimes both. The opera was already commissioned, as George had given up on the Metropolitan Opera and contracts had been signed with the Theater Guild in October of 1933.

The Metropolitan's reluctance was understandable. When money was flush, a number of American-composed operas had been mounted, all of them greeted lukewarmly and vanishing after their first season. Several had drawn their audiences largely from the participation of the great baritone, Lawrence Tibbett, and when George created the role of Porgy he thought of Tibbett in the part. But in 1933, the Depression had all but closed the Metropolitan, as wealthy patrons vanished. Otto Kahn had died, and the organization both couldn't find the money nor wanted to mount any more likely failures.

It is no accident that "Porgy," although written in the 1920's, is laid back in 1912, the year Charleston

While he was working on "Porgy and Bess" at the primitive house on Folly Island off the coast of Charleston, South Carolina, Gershwin was photographed, below top, by his cousin, the painter Henry Botkin, who provided the company George always needed even while working. He sought for "Porgy and

Bess" the director of the previous play, Rouben Mamoulian, shown at a rehearsal, bottom, with George. After some initial hesitation, because he felt protective toward the play and thought of Gershwin as primarily a Broadway composer, Mamoulian changed his mind and signed without having heard a note.

had suffered a damaging hurricane. Born in 1885, DuBose Heyward remembered it well. He also knew that by the time he wrote his novel, the special Gullah Negro life he was writing about had begun to slip away. Before the war, it had still been largely untouched.

Heyward was a Charleston aristocrat who had known early genteel poverty in a South still depressed from the Civil War. After polio had left him with a crippled arm, he had worked on the docks in the non-physical job of cargo checker. Associated daily with the black waterfront workers, the sensitive young man became fascinated with the special life of blacks who lived on and from the sea, not on the land as did most Southern blacks.

These Gullah Negroes, as they were known, had their own dialect, stories and music, particularly on certain islands adjacent to Charleston. The island Gullahs formed the nexus for "Porgy," when Heyward recalled his pre-war years among them. Already, in the post-war world, their insulated life was being eroded, and he wanted to capture it before it was gone. The year 1912 gave him the climax of his story, the hurricane, and that time was yet innocent of outside influences.

LIVING HIS WORK

Fortunately, when Gershwin came to Charleston for the summer of 1934 there was still enough to be experienced. He did not stay comfortably in Charleston but on small Folly Island, ten miles off the coast. Under the crudest conditions, with even drinking water having to be brought in, Gershwin, the New York sophisticate, happily worked. For company, he had his cousin, the painter Henry Botkin, who sketched and painted.

George seemed actually to enjoy this primitive existence, especially going to nearby larger James Island, which was heavily populated with Gullah Negroes, and because of its relative isolation still preserved much folk material. The spirituals and the complex religious improvised singing called "shouting" fascinated him. He picked up the shouting so well that at one religious meeting, as Heyward recalled, George started shouting with the congregation. He actually stole the show from their champion shouter, "probably the only white man in America who could have done that," wrote Heyward.

From these improvised, complex prayer shoutings Gershwin fashioned the hurricane scene in the opera, in which six different musical lines are interwoven. The street cries of Charleston vendors also inspired him, as the opera is laid on the Charleston

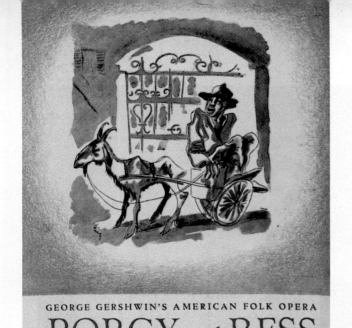

GEORGE GERSHWIN'S AMERICAN FOLK OPERA

PORGY and BESS

PRODUCTION DIRECTED BY ROUBEN MAMOULIAN

A THEATRE GUILD PRODUCTION

The Theater Guild, well aware of the importance of its sponsorship of "Porgy and Bess," had a special program cover designed for the production. Left, it featured a sketch of Porgy and his goat cart by Alexander King. Below, top, Todd Duncan, baritone and music academic, who sang the title role. Below him, right, vaudeville dancer John W. Bubbles, chosen by Gershwin for Sportin' Life although he couldn't read a note of music. Bottom left, Ruby Elzy as Serena, an impassioned leader of the chorus in such spiritual-inspired moments as the hurricane and funeral scenes.

Below, Todd Duncan as Porgy makes his triumphant return from jail into Catfish Row after having to identify the dead Crown. Bottom, he sings "I Got Plenty O' Nuthin'" in his new-found joy with Bess. Opposite page, top, the famous street vendors, selling strawberries, crabs and muffins, whose musical cries form a short

but effective opening for Act Two. Below, the rape scene on Kittiwah Island, as Crown (Warren Coleman) overcomes Bess (Anne Brown) after her initial resistance to him This scene was considered quite shocking in 1935 and was often softened in later productions.

Duncan. After a short session, he said, "Will you be my Porgy?"

Still skeptical, Duncan said he wanted to hear some of the music. After a moment's thought, Gershwin said, "This will make you famous all over the world," and began playing "I Got Plenty O' Nuthin'."

A banjo song! thought the shocked Duncan, but in a few more minutes he realized what he was hearing. Later, he was to write: "How did that wonderful man know that?"—for, indeed, the aria was to become known everywhere and to be his forever.

Anne Brown, who became Bess, simply arrived at Gershwin's apartment one day, seeking an audition. Everybody by then knew about Gershwin's pending opera. Her rendition of both spirituals and classical music caused him to take her on the spot. His casting of Sportin' Life, however, was unorthodox. He selected John W. Bubbles, then half of a successful dance team known as Buck and Bubbles. He had the personality and body moves, all right, but couldn't even read music. Teaching him note by note was so trying that even Gershwin once lost his temper and wanted to fire him. However, in the end he turned in a memorable performance and George took especial pride in him.

Despite his wish to make no compromises, Gershwin had to cut big chunks from his opera. The opening café vignette went when the Theater Guild, already terrified at the production's cost, would not pay for the extra set. Other cuts aimed at bringing the length closer to that of an ordinary Broadway show. Then there was a lot of music Gershwin had written in for Duncan in his delight at finding such a fine singer. "No one can sing that much eight times a week," he said, ever the practical man of the theater.

A DECEPTIVE SUCCESS

About a week before the opening, which was to be in Boston, Gershwin followed his practice of a run-through for an invited audience. "Porgy and Bess" was done at Carnegie Hall, in concert fashion, and was greeted with acclaim. On September 30, 1935, it opened at Boston's Colonial Theater. The audience began early in the performance to be demonstrative, and at the close, the fifteen-minute ovation reached near-pandemonium.

The Boston critics almost unanimously acclaimed "Porgy and Bess." One leading paper even published an editorial, lamenting the brief run before its departure for New York. The reaction made all the more strange the uneasy reception in New York, after the October 10th opening at the Alvin Theater. Both the drama and music critics came,

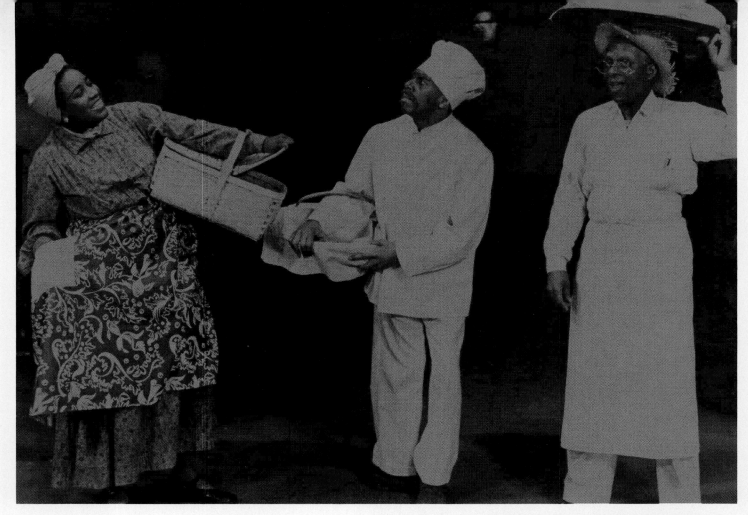

because it was on Broadway, publishing separate reviews. The drama critics liked it as a splendid translation of the play, but the music critics seemed to think they were hearing a sort of mixture of popular and serious composing.

One critic referred to the "sure-fire rubbish" of what he called the "song hits" in the score, quite forgetting that all opera composers had always injected such "hits" if they were fortunate enough to be so inspired. Another critic sneered at the very conception of the opera as "crooked folklore," as if he knew any more about Gullah Negroes than DuBose Heyward or even Gershwin, who had at least spent time in Charleston.

Even some blacks wanted to dismiss the opera. Duke Ellington, who should have known better, said that it "smacked of the conservatory and the midnight lamp"—this about a man who never went near a conservatory and knew no other method than direct experience.

In fact, Gershwin had far more experience of American black life than of any folklore of his ancestry. In rehearsals of "Porgy and Bess," it was he who showed his black singers, classically educated as they were, how to sound more "Negro!" It is notable that none of his cast ever shared these criticisms. They knew him and as J. Rosamond Johnson (Lawyer Frazier in the opera) said, they saw he had taken the often-despised "Negro" musical influence and used it for the highest expressiveness.

PORGY AND BESS

A "VERISMO" OPERA

In fact, "Porgy and Bess" stands solidly within the verismo tradition which he had grown up with, as an opera about common people leading their ordinary lives. The variety of the music, from the opening jazz piano mood scene to the final gorgeously uplifting spiritual, "Oh Lawd, I'm On My Way to a Heavenly Land," as Porgy leaves on his quest for Bess, is simply astonishing. The light-hearted aria, "A Woman is a Sometime Thing" is Gershwin's version of "La Donna è Mobile," while the two soaring love duets can be equated with Puccini's music for the lovers in the first act of "Madama Butterfly." Sportin' Life's wickedly funny "It Ain't Necessarily So" is his version of Iago's nihilistic "Credo."

The chorus in "Porgy and Bess" plays a highly im-

portant role. It is virtually a group character in the musical development, as the drama is not merely one of individual characters but of an entire community. So self-contained and vigorous is the life of Catfish Row that the intrusion of the white representatives of the law comes as a shock. Also notable is that even the spirituals, authentic-sounding as they are, were Gershwin's own compositions. The idiom is black, but the elements have been absorbed. He said himself that he had decided against using any real folk material because he wanted the score to be "all of one piece."

That score is so rich in its details that like any other masterwork it has to be heard many times before all its subtleties can be appreciated. Nor do we need today to look snobbishly down upon his deliberate use of so-called popular elements. A later critic realized this: "Gershwin's 'Porgy', like the operas of Mozart or Verdi, is at once a social act, an entertainment and a human experience with unexpectedly disturbing implications."

Above, two more scenes from the original 1935 production of "Porgy and Bess." Left, Todd Duncan, in window as Porgy, prepares to defend himself against the night sneak attack of Crown (Warren Coleman.) The photograph was posed, since the scene is actually played in near-darkness. Right, in a lighter moment, Lawyer Frazier (J. Rosamond Johnson) "divorces" Bess, even though she has never been married to Crown, for which difficult feat of law Porgy is willing to pay him $1.50.

Opposite page, the three collaborators: Heyward wrote, "For my operatic sponsor and my friend, George—with felicitations upon Porgy, and every good wish for the future," while Ira Gershwin wrote, "Dear George, in my first sentimental moment in 15 years' association with you, here's my autograph in celebration of "Porgy and Bess"—with love, Ira." This was the photograph the two presented to George after the September 30, 1935 world premiere of the opera in Boston. Above, opposite, the color program cover for the great 1952 production, showing the new Catfish Row set by Wolfgang Roth. Roth had to create the elaborate setting so it could be easily broken down and transported on tour. This production toured over four continents for four years.

Cheryl Crawford, one of the Theater Guild production staff, always believed in the opera. In 1941 she produced a revised version of "Porgy and Bess" which became the Broadway hit the first was not. Below, Georgette Harvey, the original Maria, repeated her role, but Avon Long was a new, highly acclaimed Sportin' Life. Bottom, the fishermen from this production, with Jake (Larry Matthews) left, the fisherman later drowned in the hurricane, singing "A Woman Is A Sometime Thing." This production ran through most of 1942 and was adopted by the then-new New York City Opera for the two following years.

When Gershwin died in 1937, his death notices all but ignored his opera. The "New York Times" even sniffed that "Porgy and Bess" was "innocent of elemental tragedy or real dramatic import."

However, the very next year saw a successful West Coast production, a revised version ran for eight months in New York during 1941, and the New York City Center ran this production twice in the next two years.

Although cut off from Europe by the war, "Porgy and Bess" got through, and immediately after the war began to triumph in several musical centers there, even in Moscow.

In 1945, "Porgy and Bess" was performed there by the Stanislavsky Players, and was acclaimed although only a piano and drum accompanied the performance. Dimitri Shostakovich called it "magnificent," none the less, and referred to the great Russian folk operas as its peers.

However, the most astonishing success began in 1952, when producers Blevins Davis and Robert Breen mounted a new production with two magnificent new leads. Bess was sung by the then-unknown Leontyne Price, and Porgy by William Warfield, one of the great baritones of his generation.

This production brought out the full scope of the opera, with what one New York critic called "all Gershwin and all gold . . . tempestuous . . . full of passion." The United States State Department, then funding various cultural missions, decided to send the production to Europe. It was the first time Europe had seen "Porgy and Bess" with an all-black cast, and the success would have astonished George himself.

That production was not to stop touring until 1956, visiting such unlikely places as Yugoslavia and Egypt as well as more conventional capitals, always to the same wild acclaim. Perhaps its most dramatic visit was to La Scala, the world cradle of opera, beginning February 22, 1955. "Porgy and Bess" was the first American opera to come there, the first time an American company had performed there, and the first time a single opera was repeated for a solid week.

A packed house gave the production a cheering eight-minute ovation at the final curtain. The no-

In the 1952 production young Leontyne Price sang Bess, with William Warfield as Porgy, at left. This production toured four continents. Below, Ira Gershwin at post-opening party in Vienna, with Leontyne Price, left, and Urylee Leonardos, who alternated as Bess. Bottom left, in New York, Cab Calloway, Gershwin's model for Sportin' Life, at last performed it ("It Ain't Necessarily So"). Right, the funeral scene from this production, as the poor inhabitants of Catfish Row sing "Gone, Gone, Gone" and try to fill the saucer held by Porgy (La Vern Hutcherson) with enough money for the waiting undertaker.

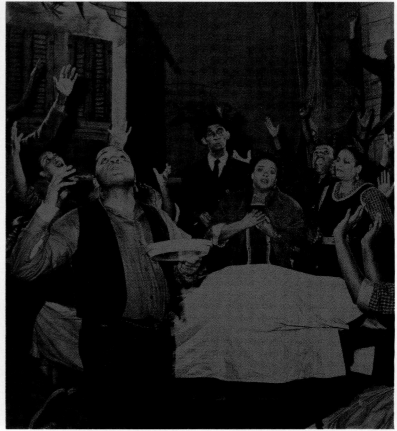

In 1959, Samuel Goldwyn released an elaborately mounted film production of "Porgy and Bess," with an all-star cast, including Sammy Davis Jr. as Sportin' Life and Dorothy Dandridge as Bess. Sydney Poitier, who played Porgy, and others, had to have singers' voices dubbed in for them. Goldwyn worried that his "highbrow" film wouldn't be a box-office success without stars known to movie audiences. Poitier was just then emerging as a black with appeal to whites. In back of him is Pearl Bailey, right, welcoming Porgy's return after being taken off to identify the dead Crown.

A MODERN SUCCESS

Grand Opera production appeared triumphantly in New York at the Uris Theater (later to be renamed the Gershwin in honor of both brothers). The production then traveled to Europe. Again using the complete score, Mr. Goldman created a new production in 1983, which made its New York appearance at Radio City Music Hall.

The Goldman/Houston stagings gave the critics a further look at "Porgy and Bess." The controversies of Gershwin's day were long dead; no critic need fear for his reputation if he praised the work. Now they compared it to such solemn twentieth century operatic icons as "Wozzeck" and "Peter Grimes." Even the once-disparaged recitatives were now praised as full of "enormous skill and subtlety."

With all this renewed and respectful attention, conductor James Levine of the Metropolitan Opera, long a champion of "Porgy and Bess," could raise again the question of his organization never having done the work. Of course, it was a very expensive new production, as no current sets or costumes could thriftily be re-used, and the entire cast would have to be specially hired except for a few principals who were, luckily, among the Met's black stars. But Levine got his way, and in 1985, its fiftieth anniversary, "Porgy and Bess" opened where Gershwin had originally dreamed that it would.

Levine was also determined to encompass the whole score. As Gershwin wrote it, "Porgy and Bess" is as long as a Wagner opera or "Der Rosenkavalier," but opera goers seldom had spent a more profitable four hours. Full houses attended, with many in the audiences obviously not regular opera goers.

The most recent production of note occurred in July, 1986 at the famed Glyndebourne Festival in England. "The New York Times" reported of the event that it was "the triumph of the operatic season." The first time "Porgy and Bess" had been done in England by a British opera entity, and the first American opera ever staged at Glyndebourne, it was conducted and directed by two leading luminaries of today, Simon Rattle and Trevor Nunn, the Royal Shakespeare Company director. The audience gave the opera a standing ovation of ten minutes, with cheers and stomping, very unlike Glyndebourne's usual polite elegance.

Sherwin M. Goldman/ Houston Grand Opera uncut production, 1976. Left middle, Larry Marshall as Sportin' Life and Clamma Dale as Bess; bottom right, Clamma Dale with Andrew Smith as Crown in the island struggle. Metropolitan Opera Production, 1985: Left, the picnic scene, with Charles Williams as Sportin' Life; bottom left, Bess (Roberta Alexander) swaggers for the Catfish Row men, including Porgy, front (Simon Estes). Below, 1986 Glyndebourne Festival production, in "Buzzard Song" scene, with Willard White's Porgy on stick crutches instead of the goat cart in the original script.

More scenes from modern productions. Right, Clamma Dale as Bess sings "I Wants to Stay Here" to Porgy (Donnie Ray Albert) in the Sherwin M. Goldman/Houston Grand Opera production. The production's picnic scene, below, short on scenery, but cleverly using lighting effects instead, as Larry Marshall sings "It Ain't Necessarily So." Bottom, from the Goldwyn film of 1959, Sydney Poitier as Porgy returns to Catfish Row after he has been detained by the police to identify Crown, whom he himself has had to kill, only to learn that Bess has gone with Sportin' Life to New York.

GERSHWIN'S STATUS TODAY

It is therefore almost unnecessary to state that "Porgy and Bess" lives today just as vividly as George Gershwin was always serenely sure it would. He was just as sure that his work for the concert hall would last, as he was always the best judge of his own composing. For him, it stood outside himself, composed, as it were, by someone else.

Successful and famous as he was in his own lifetime, he has actually continued to grow in artistic stature in the 50 years since his death. He remains among the most-performed of modern serious composers both here and abroad. He is perhaps the only twentieth century composer who continues to attract large audiences to concerts entirely of his music. New recordings come out constantly, with record stores carrying sections devoted to the many recordings which remain in active demand. In Europe and elsewhere, he is often regarded as the "only" American composer or coupled with just one other, Aaron Copland, who had also discovered that the road to effective composition lay in developing his own version of Americanism.

However, Gershwin's influence had to spread without his presence to help it. Even in his lifetime, he belonged to no coterie or school of composers. The most sociable of men, in his work he was that most American character, a loner.

Rarely and only to intimates did he show the seriousness of his commitment. When "Porgy and Bess" was running in 1935 in its initial New York production, he dropped into the theater several times a week to see some part of his beloved creation.

His friend, musicologist David Ewen, met him at a performance. Deeply impressed by the opera, Ewen said, "Now you are really beginning." He never forgot Gershwin's serious reply, "I think so, too." The tragedy was that he never had the chance to build on that great work.

With Broadway Depression-paralyzed, George and Ira looked to Hollywood. However, before leaving New York, they reverted to the old custom of interpolation, creating a satire on Viennese waltzes, "By Strauss," right, for Vincente Minelli's revue, "The Show Is On."

Gershwin's California life followed the now-familiar pattern of mixed theater and classical music activities. Below, he and Ira work in their house in Beverly Hills on the score for "Shall We Dance?"

California's outdoor life suited Gershwin's athletic temperament. Top left, opposite page, he works in the garden of his house. Around the pool gathered his many musical friends. Opposite, below, left to right, Gershwin, Harold Arlen, the song writer, and Lawrence Tibbett, the California-born Metropolitan Opera baritone.

Soon beginning to long for more serious work, Gershwin launched West Coast concerts. In January, 1937, he did three concerts with the San Francisco Symphony, then conducted by Pierre Monteux, top right opposite, who gave Gershwin his inscribed photograph. Before going to the Coast, Gershwin played his last concert at Lewisohn Stadium, July 9, 1936, for which he is shown rehearsing, bottom right opposite.

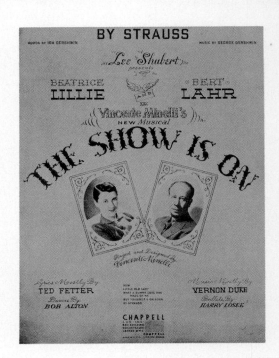

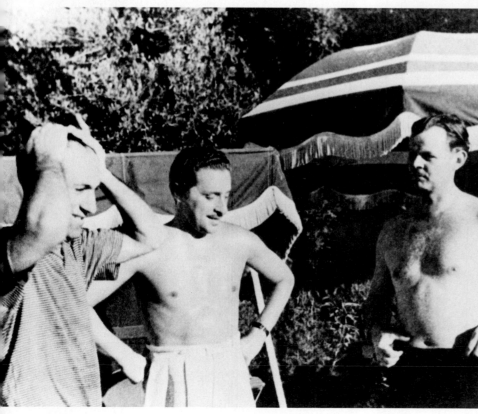

The operetta, with its fanciful European basis, clashed head-on with the brashly American musicals of George M. Cohan. Right, Victor Herbert, leader of the operetta school, in 1911, the year he also had his opera, "Natoma," produced at the Metropolitan Opera. Left below,

John Philip Sousa wrote operettas before he became the "March King." Bottom, the Four Cohans, the Nineties vaudeville act from which George M. Cohan took material for his first Broadway venture. Left to right, George, sister Josie, father Jerry and mother Nellie Cohan.

A CHANGING WORLD

While Cohan's flag-waving musicals were regularly drubbed by New York critics, they succeeded around the country, where tastes were less sophisticated. He also wrote some excellent songs for these musicals. Some of Gershwin's early songs reflect his influence in subject matter and rhythms. Below, Cohan and his longtime producer and friend, Sam H. Harris, stroll Broadway in 1904. Harris later developed his own distinguished career in the Broadway theater as a producer, and was to produce the Gershwins' "Of Thee I Sing."

Gershwin had passed from the nineteenth century through a war that had caused a revolution in morals and manners—his was, we should remember, that "Lost Generation" of Hemingway, Fitzgerald and O'Hara. Yet the man whose songs best expressed the wild confusion of that jazz-blues age, always himself seemed relatively untouched. Even today he seems vividly alive, cigar ever at a jaunty angle, always ready to play at parties, constantly composing, surrounded by loving family and admiring friends, cheerfully forging ahead in both the Broadway and concert worlds. He doesn't seem to fit with his music—but that was his secret.

When he started writing songs around 1913, the impulse arose naturally from the "Tin Pan Alley" world in which he was playing the piano. Just about everybody wrote songs—Irving Berlin couldn't read or write music and had a special keyboard on his piano which could switch key signatures for him. Many song writers came from Gershwin's own immigrant background, as if the freedom of the New World had released a pent-up desire for expression.

The New York theater around the turn of the century was dominated by "musical comedy," a new stage form based on the operettas of Vienna and Paris. They featured stories in exotic locales, with lavish scenery and costumes, and a plethora of royalty, nobility, gypsies, hussars, disguised heroines and gold-braided heroes. As George was growing up, Franz Lehar's "The Merry Widow" exemplified the form, in which Victor Herbert, Reginald De Koven and John Philip Sousa were the respected American leaders. They would be followed by Rudolf Friml, Sigmund Romberg and Herbert Stothart even into the 1920's, despite the growth of more sophisticated musicals from the Gershwins and Rodgers and Hart.

In George's boyhood, vaudeville flourished as mass entertainment. Here the native Tin Pan Alley song writer came into his own, as the technique needed for a ballad or comedy "number" was far less than that required to write an entire operetta score. In vaudeville, trained singers popularized such sentimental hits as "After the Ball is Over," and comedians set the country imitating "Mr.

A leading song writer while Gershwin was still a boy just getting a start at Remick, Irving Berlin, thirteen years older, was to become a lifelong friend and supporter of George's career. They are shown below on a Florida vacation about 1932. Back in 1916 Gershwin had brought some early songs to Berlin's publishing firm, which didn't accept them, and in 1918 he applied to be arranger and musical secretary for Berlin, who couldn't himself even read music then, despite his talent. Berlin advised him to stick with his own composing, and Gershwin took the advice.

Gallagher and Mr. Shean." At home, Americans sang Charles Wakefield Cadman's spuriously Indian "From the Land of the Sky Blue Water" and Carrie Jacobs Bond's "Mighty Lak a Rose," an example of the popular black mammy song.

If vaudeville showed black influence, as it did in songs and the use of blackface makeup by white performers, the reason was simply that vaudeville had risen from the minstrel show of the nineteenth century. Such a show featured a semicircle of blacks or whites in blackface who could each sing, dance, play banjo or tell a joke. At the center of the arc sat a master of ceremonies, always a white in full evening dress, called the Interlocutor. He played straight man for the comedians and introduced the song and dance interludes. However, the minstrel show traveled as a unit, and when theaters realized separate acts could be billed all year round, vaudeville came into being.

Vaudeville was both highly competitive and furiously creative, as the many "acts" battled to get bookings through agents. Often the performers wrote their own material and invented their own dances. Most of their material was geared to appeal to the widest mass audience, which year after year would return to see a favorite act as it came through town.

COHAN'S INFLUENCE

One of these acts was The Four Cohans, father, mother, daughter and brash son, George M. Although the act had developed a wide following, George set his sights on Broadway. Typically, his first attempt in 1901, "The Governor's Son," was expanded from his own vaudeville sketch and featured the family. From the beginning, Cohan was set against the artificiality of the dominant European operetta. He was accustomed to the Americanism of vaudeville and all his 21 musicals would be determinedly, even stridently American.

Generally, the New York critics lambasted him, and many of his shows didn't get really long runs, but on tour he found audiences loved what one New York critic disdainfully called "the pandemonium of his whole brood of musical shows." However, Cohan's "Little Johnny Jones," based on the American jockey Tod Sloan, who won the English Derby, included the songs "Yankee Doodle Dandy" and "Give My Regards to Broadway." For his "Forty-Five Minutes from Broadway" he wrote the title song and "Mary Is a Grand Old Name" and "George Washington, Jr." had "You're A Grand Old Flag." During the first World War he was to produce the enduring inspirational song, "Over There."

The cocky, aggressive George M. Cohan, left, shown at about twenty-three, continued his brashly American musicals until after World War I. The strong, thoughtful face of Gershwin, at about twenty-two, indicates the sophistication apparent from his first 1919 musical. Bottom, for one of his later films, Al Jolson lovingly recreated the oldtime minstrel show in which he had once played. The white "Mr. Interlocutor" was actor Lowell Sherman, next to whom Jolson plays a banjo. From the minstrel shows vaudeville arose.

George Gershwin loved playing and singing his own music. Only once was he caught thus by the camera, in the mid-Thirties at his Hollywood piano. Until his death in 1936, William (Bill) Daly was a valued collaborator. They are shown, bottom, in Gershwin's Riverside Drive, New York apartment, working together. The caricature of Gershwin, right, in the early Thirties, perhaps reflected his pleasure with "Of Thee I Sing." Bottom, right, Mabel Schirmer in the Twenties. She and her husband saw the triumphant London opening of "Lady, Be Good!" with George in 1926.

WORKING TOWARD A STYLE

A highly sociable personality, George Gershwin could compose amidst a hubbub of family and friends. S. N. Behrman, the playwright, recorded how in his earlier days he visited the Gershwin family house in New York and found all five floors occupied with people. He discovered George had gone around the corner to the Whitehall Hotel where he sometimes rented a suite when deadlines required uninterrupted work. He was often pursued there, too, as this photograph of 1925 shows. It was taken by a news organization, to whom George was always cordial, although he never deliberately sought publicity.

Cohan's Americanism was too simplistic for George Gershwin, but the idea that American influences could be used had certainly been implanted. As a teenager, Gershwin wrote under first one influence, then another. He found Jerome Kern very impressive on hearing his romantic song, "They Wouldn't Believe Me" from the 1913 show, "The Girl From Utah." He admired Irving Berlin from the time of Berlin's 1911 sensation, "Alexander's Ragtime Band," and occasionally in such a song as "The Real American Folk Song Is a Rag," an early collaboration with brother Ira, he seemed to be combining Berlin with George M. Cohan.

After Gershwin had left Tin Pan Alley to get into the theater, for which he now knew he would aim, it was ironic that his first real hit wasn't written for a show at all. He had had some mild success with individual numbers to interpolate in shows or be sung by stars at Sunday night concerts, and he was known to such luminaries as Sophie Tucker, Vivienne Segal, Nora Bayes and Louise Dresser. He even toured with Miss Dresser as her accompanist and with Nora Bayes when she toured in her 1918 show, "Ladies First." She was using a couple of his songs, and wanted him to change them to suit her style. Although usually amenable to such changes, and only a relatively unknown twenty-year-old, George answered calmly, "I like it the way it is." The usually imperious Miss Bayes couldn't budge him.

The odd thing about Gershwin's first great song hit, "Swanee," was that it forecast nothing of the mature Gershwin style. It was born out of casual conversation with Irving Caesar, who had already written lyrics for other Gershwin songs, about doing something like "Hindustan," then a popular song. They thought they ought to use an American locale, which suggested Stephen Foster's classic "Swanee River."

However, Gershwin's and Caesar's "Swanee" turned out to be nothing like Foster's sentimental ballad. After its inauspicious debut in the stage show for the opening of the Capitol Theater, a motion-picture palace, when producer Ned Wayburn enthusiastically sank the rollicking tune under over-production, it seemed destined for oblivion. Gershwin's habit of playing his own music

Ira Gershwin, below, two years older than George, was completely different in personality, yet no composer-lyricist team ever worked in greater harmony. The brothers lived their own lives, yet always in close proximity, and their admiration for each other's work was noted by all who knew them even casually. After "Lady, Be

Good!" their collaboration continued, particularly with the musical, "Oh, Kay!" of 1926 for Gertrude Lawrence, bottom with leading man Oscar Shaw. "Oh, Kay!" was written especially for her, after her New York debut in "Charlot's Revue" had given her instant Broadway acclaim.

Man I Love" was written. The decision to pull it out may have been right, as it may not have fit the mood of a show with the two dancing Astaires. "Fascinating Rhythm," so intricate that Ira on first hearing it demanded to know how anyone could write a lyric to it, was exactly right. The show also gave both brothers scope for the humor they loved. Gershwin's earliest efforts had included humorous songs, such as "When You Want 'Em You Can't Get 'Em (When You Got 'Em You Don't Want 'Em)," his first published song, which had attracted star Sophie Tucker.

Subsequently, his songs for interpolation by stars into their shows often had a humorous bent, such as "Do It Again" for the French singer Irene Bordoni in her 1922 show, "The French Doll." George and Ira would write songs just for private parties, such as "Mischa, Jascha, Toscha, Sascha," a humorous description of the careers of the four greatest violinists of the time, Mischa Elman, Jascha Heifetz, Toscha Seidel and Sascha Jacobson, one or more of whom would be at such a party.

In their casually offbeat way of looking at life, George and Ira were in total sympathy, although their characters were highly unlike. George was furiously energetic, ever working or going to parties, a ladies' man. Ira was slow-moving, very reticent, not prone to work unless pushed, placid and content with home life. Their very differences seemed to make them fit together all the better, each supplying what the other needed.

Certainly, George Gershwin's career cannot be separated from Ira. In fact, it could even be said that he was more dependent upon Ira than Ira was upon him, as Ira often wrote just as successfully for other composers. Without him, however, George's work tended to be uneven. Ira's ideas stimulated Gershwin as did no other lyricist.

Ira didn't set out to be a lyricist, in the way that George singlemindedly determined to become a composer. He wanted to write, but as his talent from the beginning seemed to be for those ephemeral bits of prose or verse that in those days could get into certain specialized columns in newspapers, he apparently had little prospect of making a living. But his juvenile scrapbooks show an intense inter-

In 1925 the two Gershwins had written a musical, "Tip-Toes", for a star very different from Miss Lawrence. Left, Queenie Smith, in a scene from "Tip-Toes." The musical's big jazz number went to her co-star, Andrew Toombes, as she was a ballet-trained dancer-singer. Below, Gertrude Lawrence and star comedian Victor Moore in a scene from "Oh, Kay!" Disguised as servants in a millionaire's home, they sang "Ain't It Romantic." Typical of the era, "Oh, Kay!" had an inconsequential "book." Bottom, publicity photograph of the show's three stars.

Gershwin was always a genial collaborator with other talents. In 1928 he co-wrote the score for "Rosalie," produced by Florenz Ziegfeld, left below, with Sigmund Romberg, right, who had used one of George's early songs in 1916 in a show he composed. Romberg led the operetta school of com- posers in the 1920's. Right, Jack Donahue and Marilyn Miller, the show's stars. At bottom, backstage with, left to right, Donahue, Miller, Gershwin, Romberg and Ziegfeld. Gershwin's songs for this musical were of the bouncy, light-hearted kind, with Romberg supplying the romantic numbers.

In the 1920's, ballet-trained Marilyn Miller was the idol of the Broadway musical theater. She had first been noticed in "revues," shows which were Broadway versions of vaudeville, with more sophisticated skits, performers, singers and dancers. In the Twenties, when Florenz Ziegfeld began producing "book" musicals, with librettos, Miller became his favorite star. She signed this photograph, below, to Gershwin, at the time of "Rosalie." Like him, she was to die prematurely in the 1930's, after her last show, the successful revue, "As Thousands Cheer."

est in words and the way they can be put together for effects.

He wrote his first song lyrics in 1917, when he was already 21, whereas George at a much earlier age had begun writing songs. Although these first lyrics were for two of George's early songs, Ira worked with other song writers as his career in music grew. Evidently, it wasn't obvious to the brothers that they were a foreordained combination.

After "Lady, Be Good!" the fact certainly was obvious. The brothers worked so closely that no particular method of composition dominated the partnership. Sometimes George came up first with the music, perhaps developed from the many ideas he dashed down in his notebooks all the time. Sometimes as they talked, they developed words and music together. Often Ira's provocative ideas, titles, phrases or word interest inspired Gershwin to the musical setting.

Ira said himself that George was original and distinctive in "musicalizing words." The result was always a song in which words and music were particularly inseparable. Ira's genius lay in his seemingly offhand way of using common speech: "I'm bidin' my time," "Let's call the whole thing off," "They all laughed," or "It's all bananas." Together, the Gershwins produced a song style deceptively casual even when tackling subjects like love, usually then treated with conventional sentiments and equally sugary music. Instead, Ira wrote, "They're writing songs of love, but not for me . . . I was a fool to fall and get That Way," and George's music to such rueful lines was in the same mood.

Beyond the songs themselves, the Gershwins pushed steadily against the conventions of musical comedy. The Broadway theater then housed a mixture of European-style operetta, musicals tailored for stars and a few newly sophisticated works. George's first show, "La, La, Lucile," had been firmly in the last genre. Its book and songs treated matrimony and divorce with a light hand still quite daring in 1919.

George was always to do his best work with such shows and with the new breed of star: Gertrude Lawrence, Ginger Rogers, Ethel Merman. The

The 1920's saw a lively mixture of musical types in the New York theater. Richard Rodgers, seen below, left, with his lyricist Lorenz Hart, wrote for revues and "book" shows, particularly the pioneering "A Connecticut Yankee," with its story from Mark Twain's book. They mixed archaic English in their songs with the kind of modern Americanisms the Gershwins had already used for "Tip-Toes," whose stars, Queenie Smith and Andrew Toombes, are seen at bottom. This musical also had an American plot, about stranded vaudevillians involved in the Florida land boom.

Astaires were dancers, not singers, who put over songs by their personal style. None of these 1920's stars fit the pre-War mold of sentimental or "romantic" personalities.

George's scores for the musicals which still tried to repeat pre-War styles were always less successful. Out of "Our Nell," "Sweet Little Devil," "Song of the Flame," and "Rosalie," only the last made a hit. Perhaps the incandescent Marilyn Miller, the one musical star who seems to have enchanted everyone then, was responsible, but there was also the fact that George didn't have to write the gushier parts of the score. Sigmund Romberg did the "romantic" numbers, so George could concentrate on the more lighthearted "Say So!," "Oh Gee! Oh Joy!" and "How Long Has This Been Going On?"

IMPROVING THE BREED

If the Gershwins were leading the way, other Broadway musical writers were close behind. In fact, 1927 was a banner year, when George and Ira created "Funny Face" for the Astaires, Jerome Kern created the first American operetta in "Show Boat" and Richard Rodgers teamed with Lorenz Hart as his lyricist for "A Connecticut Yankee." The last was as American as "Show Boat," both having been taken from recognized literary works. Lorenz Hart pulled off a very Ira-like lyric in "Thou Swell," with modern slang and archaic English mixed for a love song.

But at a time when a couple of hundred Broadway plays and musicals still crowded the stage, overall progress was spotty. "Funny Face" itself suffered from a book so silly that it was regarded as a failure in its out-of-town tryouts and went through a frantic period of revisions, including a change of title before the groggy cast discovered to their astonishment after the Broadway opening that they had a hit.

It was the music, with Ira's lyrics, that did it. People in that era went to a musical for the music, the production and the performers. At its best, the book was often simply an excuse to get from song to

The Twenties musical mixture included a revival of "The Chocolate Soldier," an operetta from 1911, kept fresh by its plot from George Bernard Shaw's satire, "Arms and the Man." Left, George Gershwin visited backstage: left to right, Gershwin, the revival's star, Wilbur Evans, composer Oskar Straus.

Below, left and bottom, Fred and Adele Astaire in scenes from "Funny Face," the Gershwin brothers' 1927 musical. Below, right, the only relic of "Treasure Girl," the 1928 failure for Gertrude Lawrence, is this photograph, one of only two now known to exist of her with Gershwin.

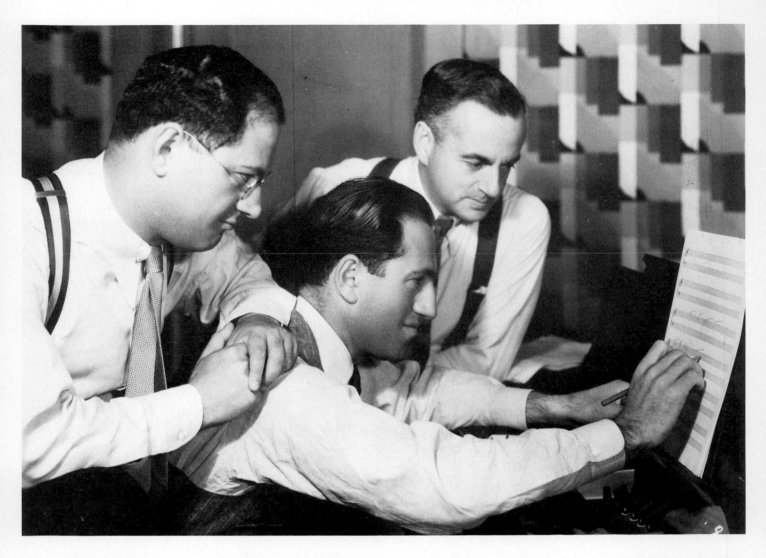

In 1930, the Gershwins accomplished a rarity in musical theater, a successful second version of a previously failed show. "Strike Up The Band" had never even reached Broadway in 1927, but now ran 191 performances at the Alvin Theater. Opposite page, top, the star comic team of Bobby Clark, left, and Paul McCullough with ladies of the chorus. Below, opposite, romantic leads Gordon Smith and Doris Carson. An anti-war satire, the show contained the politically humorous songs George and Ira liked to write. The success encouraged them and writers George S. Kaufman and Morrie Ryskind to conceive

another satirical show. The same year, the Gershwins opened their lampoon of the Westerns so popular in films of the day, "Girl Crazy." They had worked with skilled librettist Guy Bolton before, who had also collaborated with English writer P. G. Wodehouse on successful musicals. Above, this page, left to right, Ira Gershwin, George Gershwin and Guy Bolton. Previous successes with Bolton had included a London musical, "Primrose," never seen here, "Lady, Be Good!", "Tip-Toes," "Oh, Kay!" and "Rosalie." However, the production of "Girl Crazy" was to be the Gershwins' last collaboration with Bolton.

dance to song. Always a prolific composer, Gershwin never minded dropping numbers, replacing even a good song with another or adding a new one altogether when a performer couldn't handle what he had written or wasn't right for the song.

In 1924 he wrote "The Man I Love" for his first Astaire show, "Lady, Be Good!" but pulled it out when it didn't seem to suit Adele Astaire's pert personality. However, he knew the song was good and in 1927 he tried to use it in the first version of "Strike Up The Band!" Again, it didn't work, nor yet for a third show, "Rosalie." Fortunately, "The Man I Love" had been published in sheet music, an autographed copy of which Lady Louis Mountbatten received from Gershwin when she heard the song at parties in New York. From that one copy, which she gave to her favorite London club orchestra, "The Man I Love" became a London and Paris hit before it was taken up at home by orchestras and singer Helen Morgan, its ideal interpreter.

Gershwin once said that his difficulties with the song came from its construction, which plays off a minor-key six-note progression against a descending chromatic scale background. It was a singer's

song, not a tune to whistle casually. One might add that unlike many blues songs, it has a spare nobility rather than sentimentalism—compare it, for example, to "My Man," an embarrassingly weepy number sung by Fanny Brice for many years.

After "Lady, Be Good!" George Gershwin wrote no less than three musicals in the one year of 1925. Significantly, only one was written entirely with Ira and was a hit, "Tip-Toes." The brothers produced the wry love song, "Looking For a Boy," the blues-influenced "That Certain Feeling" and "Sweet and Low Down," the last as jazzy a number as Gershwin ever conceived.

The Gershwins turned to writing "Oh, Kay!" for Gertrude Lawrence. Lawrence was then a star new to Broadway, who had made a hit in 1924 when she came over with the London show, "Charlot's Revue." American producers pursued her to star in an American musical, and when Aarons & Freedley said that George Gershwin would write their musical for her, she at once accepted their offer.

The coming show aroused so much interest that at the later rehearsals the Music Box Theater filled up every morning with Gershwin and Lawrence ad-

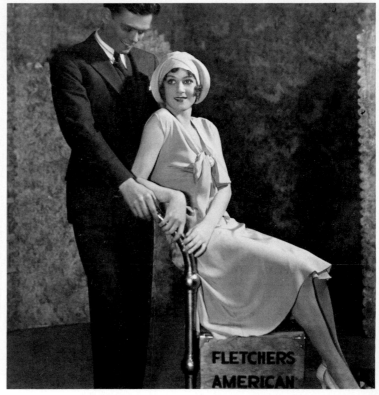

In this same period, Ira and George Gershwin went West themselves for the first time, signed to create a musical film for Fox stars Janet Gaynor and Charles Farrell. Right, Gaynor as a naive Scottish immigrant in "Delicious," imagines her welcome to the United States with a whole chorus of "Uncle Sams." Gershwin expanded music written for "Delicious" into his "Second Rhapsody." Bottom, Ginger Rogers became a star in "Girl Crazy" as the postmistress romantic lead. With her, a male quartet of "cowboys," who sang "Bidin' My Time," the Gershwins' celebration of leisurely country life.

partment chairman at the University of California at Los Angeles (UCLA). Pleased at the university's action in sheltering Schoenberg, George offered "Strike Up the Band" to UCLA for its school song at football games. Ira wrote new words for it, and it was formally presented to the university in Royce Hall, with George at the piano. Few colleges can boast of so distinguished a march.

The entire score for "Strike Up the Band" was geared to expressing the satiric thrust of the book rather than to creating individual song hits. While the minor-key ballad "Soon" certainly did become a hit, and "I've Got a Crush on You" charmed with its casual warmth, more typical was the humorous irony of "A Typical Self-made American," "If I become the President" and "The Unofficial Spokesman." The integration of book and music took a big step forward in George and Ira's aims for the musical theater.

SPOOFING THE WESTERN

"Strike Up the Band" wasn't as big a hit as the next Gershwin musical, its 191 performances not coming near the 272 which "Girl Crazy" was to rack up. That musical was an example of the magic which only occasionally descends upon every aspect of a show. It started with the book, less trenchant than the political satire of "Strike Up the Band," but a parody, nonetheless, of the then-popular Westerns in movies. Just as "Strike Up the Band" had been preceded by "The Chocolate Soldier," fashioned by Viennese composer Oscar Strauss from George Bernard Shaw's anti-war satire, "Arms and the Man," so the Western spoof had already been the basis for "Whoopee," starring Eddie Cantor.

However, the idea was still good, especially in the comic hands of Willie Howard as a Jewish New York taxi driver trying to go Western. Even more memorable were its two female leads. One was Ginger Rogers, who sang two of the best of all Gershwin romantic songs, "Embraceable You" and "But Not For Me." The other was almost unknown, a girl who

The memory of "Girl Crazy" is still green especially for the emergence of Ethel Merman, below in a scene from the musical. Then twenty-two, she came equipped by nature with a trumpet-like voice that could hold the longest, loudest high note ever heard, in "I Got Rhythm." It was to be her lifelong signature song, although she was never again to appear in a Gershwin musical. Her last service for George was to sing at the memorial concert held in Lewisohn Stadium in August, 1937. After Gershwin, she starred in musicals by Cole Porter and Irving Berlin.

AND NOW ETHEL MERMAN

had filled only one important stage engagement so far. Gershwin had three numbers for her.

That girl, who was to be star Ethel Merman, was nearly paralyzed by a solo audition for Gershwin. He liked her and at once played for her the songs he had in mind for her role. Mistaking her feeble comments for disapproval, George kept assuring her, with his customary adaptability, that he would change whatever she didn't like. This flustered the tyro even more, who could only gulp, "They'll do very nicely, Mr. Gershwin." Her friends found this response hilarious, naturally, but Merman just couldn't think of anything else to say.

At any rate, there was no shyness about her on opening night when she let loose with "I Got Rhythm," especially when, in the second chorus, she held a high C for sixteen trumpet-like bars against the melody by the orchestra. Her other numbers were "Sam and Delilah," a parody of the heavy seduction style often seen in movies of the day, and "Boy! What Love Has Done to Me!," a rollicking piece of Gershwin humor that pulled no stops on the usually sentimental subject of misfortune in love.

"I Got Rhythm" is unusual not only for its changing rhythms but for the rising and falling five-note melody from the pentatonic scale. The lyric is very simple, as it has to be with that music, even repeating the famous line "Who could ask for anything more?" four times. Ira must have liked it, because he was to use it in two later songs; perhaps it had even for him the particular Gershwin magic.

Ira also liked "Bidin' My Time," which George wrote for a cowboy quartet in "Girl Crazy" to express the slow pace of country life. Ira had picked up that phrase way back in 1916, and now it came in handy. One can also still laugh at a song titled "When It's Cactus Time in Arizona," parodying all those songs dripping romance on various lusher locales.

The final triumph of the Gershwins on Broadway arose not from "Girl Crazy," however, but from "Strike Up the Band." A new musical was to satirize domestic politics as the first had skewered international diplomacy and war-making. The team was even the same, as George S. Kaufman did the book,

The satire in "Of Thee I Sing" spared no target, from the conduct of political campaigns to the Supreme Court. The total uselessness of Vice Presidents, true of that time, was pointed up in the scene at left, where Victor Moore as V.P. Alexander Throttlebottom (hat in hand) appears among a group of tourists about to enter the White House. It's the only way he can get in. Below, the First Lady (Lois Moran) saves President Wintergreen (William Gaxton) from impeachment by having twins. As Throttlebottom notes, the country has never yet impeached an expectant President.

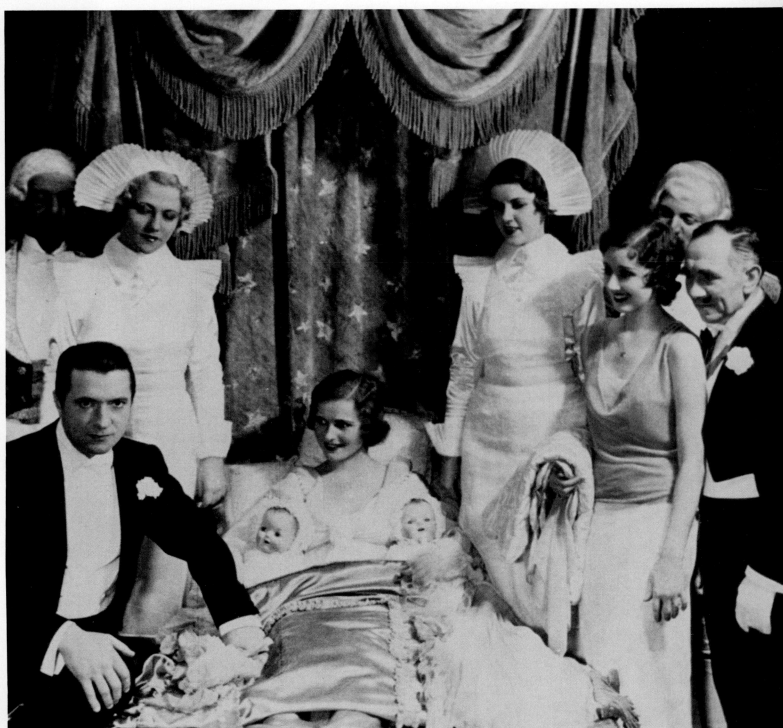

During these years, the much-pictured Gershwins came under the caricaturist's pen of the great Al Hirschfeld, whose drawing of the two brothers, shown here, became their most-reproduced image down to modern times. Hirschfeld caught perfectly the nuances of the brothers' personalities.

HIRSCHFELD

this time with Morrie Ryskind as collaborator from the beginning.

If "Of Thee I Sing" has proven unrevivable, it is precisely because it was so topical in its time. It was created just before the electronic media altered politics forever—Franklin D. Roosevelt, who was to use radio so effectively, wasn't even elected until the year after the musical, which opened in 1931. So the musical begins with a then-traditional torchlight parade for Wintergreen, the show's presidential candidate.

Not that some of Ira's lyrics aren't applicable today. In the parade's chant, "Wintergreen for President," occurs such lines as "Loves the Irish and the

Jews," to George's musical suggestions of both ethnic strains. As for a campaign issue, politicians today are still searching for themes that will rouse the voters without offending anybody—in the musical, the only one they can think of is—love.

This leads to a beauty contest, still to be found all over the land. Wintergreen is that unacceptable thing politically, a bachelor. He will marry the contest winner. Unfortunately, he falls for another girl entirely. No liberated woman she, but the perfect cook. As the contest winner has French connections, this leads to international complications, even a projected impeachment of Wintergreen after his election, with opportunity for satirizing the Sen-

ate and even the Supreme Court.

While all of this sounds fairly modern, the role of
the Vice President as a perfect nonentity no longer
applies. At the time, however, this role, including a
scene where he gets into the White House only by
joining a tourist group, was hilarious. The
Gershwins didn't even mind poking fun at canned
patriotism, in the title song, "Of Thee I
Sing—Baby," blithely throwing out such blather in
favor of a jaunty paean to the heroine of the story.
Although both Gershwins sought to create a musical with a seamless wedding of book, lyrics and
music, George couldn't help coming up with a couple of lilting individual song hits: "Love Is Sweep-
ing the Country" and "Who Cares?" The latter was
to be one of the Gershwin songs that George Balanchine included for his 1970 ballet, which also carried it as the ballet's title, "Who Cares?"

To the sensation caused by the musical was added
the Pulitzer Prize for drama, awarded to Kaufman,
Ryskind and Ira Gershwin as co-authors of the text.
This was the first time a Pulitzer had been given to a
musical comedy text, and the citation stated, "This
award may seem unusual, but the play is unusual."
Unfortunately, George couldn't get a prize for what

---

*Hirschfeld also created a famous group caricature,
"American Popular Song: The Songwriters." At
the keyboard, left to right, Duke Ellington, George
Gershwin and Hoagy Carmichael. Around them,
clockwise from left: Richard Rodgers, Lorenz
Hart, Cole Porter, Harold Arlen, Dorothy Fields,
Jerome Kern, Johnny Mercer, Ira Gershwin and
Irving Berlin.*

is, after all, the major point of any musical, as Pulitzer prizes were not then awarded to music. However, any triumph of one brother was always regarded with pleasure by the other, so both George and Ira could console themselves with that Pulitzer when the year of 1933 produced not only the failure of "Let 'Em Eat Cake," but the even more dismal failure of "Pardon My English," which the brothers had been reluctant to do from the first.

THE LAST MUSIC

Three years passed before Gershwin again turned to theater music, and now it was for films. He didn't particularly care for film work, remembering well from his first venture how a composer was simply a paid hand with no control over the finished film. He had also come away from two years of the most strenuous creative effort of his life, "Porgy and Bess." Having made that giant stride, could he turn again to the lighter work of songs for what amounted to theater?

However, Gershwin's habit of constant piano improvisation hadn't ceased, opera or no opera. Even for "Let 'Em Eat Cake" he had produced one song which has entered the canon of his major work, "Mine," and not long before he left for Hollywood in 1936, he had improvised a take-off on sugary Viennese waltzes which he and Ira turned into "By Strauss" for interpolation in the Broadway revue, "The Show Is On." Gene Kelly was to re-use this number in the film, "An American in Paris."

At least, on the new Hollywood venture he would be writing for two old friends, Fred Astaire and Ginger Rogers. Although the book of "Shall We Dance?" harked back to trite musical comedy formulas, the scope for varied composing was there. Scarcely a number in that film wasn't classic Gershwin, from the comic jazz of "Slap That Bass" to the wit of "Let's Call the Whole Thing Off" and "They All Laughed." The typically wry Gershwin approach to thwarted love is expressed in "They Can't Take That Away From Me." In his music for the obligatory big Rogers-Astaire dance duet, "Shall We Dance," he produced another of his broad "noble" melodies, but this time quite without Tschaikovskian overtones.

"A Damsel in Distress," which followed immediately in early 1937, was all Astaire, as he had a new leading lady, Joan Fontaine, who was no dancer. But the story was a lot better, a light farce by P. G. Wodehouse, who wrote the screenplay. Its comic elements suited George and Ira just fine, as they proved in their satire of amateur English madrigal groups, "The Jolly Tar and the Milkmaid." They also produced the jaunty "Things Are Looking Up"

In "Let 'Em Eat Cake" (1933), Depression cynicism sparks this scene, opposite bottom, of Phillip Loeb singing "Down With Everything That's Up." Even the three stars, below, repeating their roles from "Of Thee I Sing" (William Gaxton, Lois Moran and Victor Moore), couldn't recreate the earlier success. Audiences preferred cheerful Fred Astaire-Ginger Rogers movie musicals. They appear opposite, center, in the title number of "Shall We Dance?" and left on roller skates for "Let's Call the Whole Thing Off." Astaire, opposite, in "A Damsel in Distress," with George Burns and Gracie Allen.

---

and the classic "Nice Work If You Can Get It," which put the expression itself into the language.

The best number for many Gershwin lovers was produced by George in less than an hour expressly for Fred Astaire to sing in a "walking" scene. "A Foggy Day in London Town" was simply sung as Astaire walked and lightly danced through a half-sunny, half-misty woodland. Although in Gershwin's characteristic casual mood, it was written with a longer line, a legato flow that almost over-taxed the very light voice of Fred Astaire, who got away with the ending upward inflection only by slightly faking it. Even so, it is indelibly associated with him.

Although George was eager to get back to New York, his natural stamping ground, he allowed producer Samuel Goldwyn to entice him for one more picture score. The film was to be called "The Goldwyn Follies," in an obvious attempt to match in film the kind of show for which Ziegfeld was noted. Again, George would be writing individual numbers, not a real score, but in May, 1937, he began the job as soon as he had finished with "A Damsel in Distress."

Goldwyn always provided everything of the best, so Alfred Newman was to conduct and a choreographer then just on the verge of fame was to do the dances. It was George Balanchine, then thirty-three years old and a theater craftsman after the Gershwins' own heart. George was soon fired up with the idea of composing a ballet for Balanchine to choreograph in the film, but he didn't live to write it.

However, Gershwin finished five songs before late June, when the rapidly growing brain tumor incapacitated him. Of these, two are among his masterpieces. One is "Love Walked In," in his legato melodious vein, with just that light touch in Ira's lyrics to save it from sentimentalism: "My heart seemed to know that love said 'Hello'!" and the sudden changes which give George's late songs their individuality, as on the next line: "Though not a word was spoken."

George Gershwin enjoyed his second Hollywood stay better than his first, partly because many musician and composer friends were also there. Below, Dimitri Tiomkin left, and Charles Previn, working on a movie score. Previn had conducted George's 1934 concert tour, and Tiomkin had been the first Europe-an pianist to play the "Concerto in F," with George in the audience (1928). Bottom, Gershwin with Jerome Kern, in a Hollywood studio. Right, a portrait session in his Hollywood house included this shot of him with his secretary, Nanette Kutner.

George Gershwin was working on a third film, "The Goldwyn Follies," when he died. As always, producer Samuel Goldwyn had only the best talent for his film. Below, George Balanchine, then struggling to establish his ballet career in America, was the choreographer, as he often worked for Hollywood and Broadway. Gershwin and he planned a ballet for the film, but Gershwin died before he could write the music. Bottom, Gershwin's friend, Vernon Duke, who finished "The Goldwyn Follies" after Gershwin's untimely death.

The other song, "Our Love Is Here to Stay" is unusually tender in the melody, played against a lyric which actually dares to begin with a verse referring to the shaky state of the world. Every nuance of Ira's lines is followed, as in the couplet: "In time the Rockies may crumble, Gibraltar may tumble," with its shrug of an afterthought: "They're only made of clay."

Recently, the Gershwin sister, Frances, who had a brief singing career in the 1920's, sang this song on a television program about George. In her treatment, the song became a tribute to him. Despite his absorption in music, George had always been a warmly affectionate man, and fifty years after his death, the song he wrote almost at his end perhaps expresses himself best of all.

WHAT MAKES A GERSHWIN SONG?

Except for the uncharacteristic "Swanee," George Gershwin was not really a popular song composer. Although everyone recognized a Gershwin song when they heard it, his work seldom lent itself to easy reproduction. In his time, it was recognized that Broadway music had to be several cuts above "Tin Pan Alley" songs, and with the sophisticated lyrics his brother wrote for him, the results were for trained singers and orchestras to play.

Gershwin never allowed the first inspiration to work itself out conventionally. He would change keys, use an unusual harmony or even a contrapuntal theme in the orchestra. It cannot be emphasized too strongly that he was not a "jazz" composer. He used jazz elements, as he used blues, along with his own melodic inspirations, to create his unique style.

From beginning to end, the Gershwin songs were characterized by a seeming spontaneity which is still theirs if rightly interpreted. Attempts to apply frills to them don't work. They come from American popular idioms, but they are in their own right as classic as the songs of composers from other backgrounds, particularly Schubert, to whom critics today do not hesitate to compare him.

106

*The head of George Gershwin,
sculpted by Isamu Noguchi,
1929, in a brooding portrait of genius.*

ACKNOWLEDGMENTS

Without the generous aid of many individuals, this book could not have been completed. My gratitude goes first to members of the Gershwin family: Mrs. Frances Gershwin Godowsky, Mrs. Arthur (Judy) Gershwin, Mrs. Ira (Leonore) Gershwin and Mr. Marc Gershwin. Mrs. Mabel Schirmer also generously permitted photographing of her special Gershwin items.

The collections of a number of institutions were invaluable, with the unfailing helpfulness of their curators and research aides. I should like particularly to express my appreciation to: Wayne Shirley of the Music Division of the Library of Congress, Dorothy Swerdlove of the Billy Rose Collection at the New York Public Library at Lincoln Center, Lisa Onofri of the Theater Collection at the Museum of the City of New York, Terry Ariano of the Photo Lab at the Museum of the City of New York, Helen Harrison of the Guild Hall, Easthampton, Long Island and Jeffrey S. Mintz of the Academy of Motion Picture Arts and Sciences.

My thanks go to my photographers, credited below, who often had to shoot their photos under difficult conditions, and to the expertise and patient work of Albert Karsten, the book's designer. Last but not least, to my husband, appreciation is due for his support during the many months of work and his assistance in obtaining out-of-the-way items.

BIBLIOGRAPHY

Appelbaum, Stanley, ed.—*The New York Stage: Famous Productions in Photographs.* New York: Dover Publications, Inc., 1976.
Armitage, Merle—*George Gershwin.* New York: Longmans, Green & Co., 1938.
Armitage, Merle—*George Gershwin, Man and Legend.* New York: Duell, Sloan and Pierce, 1958. Reprint, 1970, Books for Libraries Press, Freeport, New York.
Astaire, Fred—*Steps in Time.* New York: Harper & Row, 1959.
Baragwanath, Albert K.—*New York Life at the Turn of the Century in Photographs.* New York: Dover Publications, Inc., 1985.
Engel, Lehman—*The American Musical Theater/A Consideration.* New York: A CBS Legacy Collection Book, distributed by the MacMillan Company, 1967.
Ewen, David—*George Gershwin: His Journey to Greatness.* New York: Prentice-Hall, 1970; revised and re-issued 1986 by The Ungar Publishing Company, New York.
Goldberg, Isaac—*George Gershwin.* New York: Simon and Schuster, 1931; supplemented by Edith Garson and re-issued 1958 by Frederick Ungar Publishing Co.

Hingham, John—*Send These To Me: Jews and Other Immigrants in Urban America.* New York: Atheneum, 1975.
Jablonski, Edward and Stewart, Lawrence D.—*The Gershwin Years.* New York: Doubleday & Co., 1958. Revised 1973.
Kimball, Robert and Simon, Alfred—*The Gershwins.* New York: Atheneum, 1973.
Merman, Ethel—*Who Could Ask For Anything More?* New York: Doubleday & Co., 1955.
Moore, MacDonald Smith—*Yankee Blues—Musical Culture and American Identity.* Bloomington, Ind.: Indiana University Press, 1985.
Schwartz, Charles—*Gershwin: His Life and Music.* Indianapolis: Bobbs-Merrill Co., 1973 (Da Capo Reprint).
Stearns, Marshall—*The Story of Jazz.* New York: a Mentor Book, 1956.
Thomson, Virgil—*American Music Since 1900.* New York: Holt, Rinehart & Winston, 1971.
Toll, Robert C.—*Blacking Up: The Minstrel Show in Nineteenth-Century America.* London: Oxford University Press, 1974.

Above—Glyndebourne Festival set, showing chorus in early Catfish Row morning scene. Right—Sammy Davis, Jr. singing "It Ain't Necessarily So," Samuel Goldwyn film production, 1959.